Urban Shalom & the Cities We Need

Edited by Andre Van Eymeren,
Ash Barker, Bryan McCabe
& Chris Elisara

Urban Shalom & the Cities We Need

First published 2017

Published by Urban Shalom Publishing

28 Handsworth New Rd, Birmingham B18 4PT, UK

Editors: Andre Van Eymeren, Ash Barker, Bryan McCabe & Chris Elisara

Cover Design & Typesetting: Amynoel Van Eymeren

Printer: Ingram's Lightning Source

Urban Shalom & the Cities We Need

ISBN 978-1-9997798-9-4

Contents

Introduction

"There comes a point where we need to stop just pulling people out of the river. We need to go upstream and find out why they're falling in."
Desmond Tutu

Currently at least 3.5 billion people (half the world's population) live in an urban environment. This is set to rise dramatically over the next 30 years, and by the time 2050 rolls around at least two-thirds of the world's population will be living in cities. Whether you live in a city, a suburb, or a rural area how the world's cities are designed, grow, and develop over the next three decades will have a major bearing on your life and that of your family. How urban areas develop will also effect creation, the economy, our communities, churches, and our spiritual lives.

In Quito, October 2016, over 45,000 global leaders gathered for UN Habitat III to talk about the future of cities and to launch the New Urban Agenda, a document that sets the tone for the development of cities for the next twenty years. Many of the writers of this book also convened there with other Christians from around the world to explore this theme as part of *The Gospel and the Future of Cities Summit.* We discussed a broad spectrum of urban challenges and opportunities, and how we can respond from a biblical perspective, as a people of God. We then became a delegation into the Habitat III conversations to learn and be a Christian witness into this historic event. As a Christian delegation, we became committed to not only the heart behind the agenda but to how the community of faith can play a part in its implementation both globally and at a local level.

The conference was the culmination of a UN Habitat led process that included over 100,000 participants over three years and pointed to the

Quito event where all the participating nations voted to adopt the New Urban Agenda. World Evangelical Alliance/Lausanne Creation Care Network and Micah Global's International Society for Urban Mission (changing its name to Urban Shalom Society, USS) were behind bringing the Christian delegation together.

The world 's commitment to the positive spirit of the New Urban Agenda is so important because it recognizes the very real sustainability and inequality challenges we face as a planet. The commitment also demonstrates the belief that if we work together cities can become solutions to these issues. As Christians, we affirm the New Urban Agenda as it creates a space for us to work together with all people, institutions and governments around the world. However, we also want our faith communities to go deeper and further. God's call for us to is seek the shalom of the city where we live and to pray to the Lord on its behalf because in its shalom we will find our shalom. This means people living in a deep harmony with God, each other and the place they live. Such a vision becoming a reality through God's power benefits all and leaves no one behind. Faith communities have a responsibility to focus on this deeper urban agenda as well as joining with others in understanding and implementing the UN's New Urban Agenda.

The world's commitment to the New Urban Agenda is the start, not the end, of the process for building sustainable, just, and liveable cities for all. *This is a significant step forward, but the most important steps are still before us, namely the implementation. The Christian community around the world needs to be involved, and we hope this book and the Urban Shalom Project will be key catalysts to help the faith community understand and work with other towards the realization of the New Urban Agenda, albeit from a distinctly Christian perspective and means.*

To help Christians become more aware and engaged in the New Urban Agenda and the *Cities We Need* document, a key thematic tool arising from twenty-six Urban Thinkers Campuses held around the world in the lead up to Habitat III. The Urban Shalom Project will launch a Call to

Urban Action Campaign, (details of the call to action is in the concluding chapter), this book, as well, we will host and co-host various processes, forums and events with partners around the world.

We Need to Engage an Urban Theology

Through our time in Quito we recognized that the world is rapidly changing and is challenging the very nature of Christian faith and mission, with significant implications for Christian discipleship which is effected by how and where people live together. In 1800 only 3% of people lived in cities, but now more than half of all humans live in urban environments with over one third facing severe urban poverty. With the expected growth of urbanization the current levels of disparity, diversity and density will only increase leaving no person, place or culture untouched.

We recognize that areas of urban deprivation and poverty are especially complex places to make a long-term impact, but they are some of the most critical frontline contexts for Christian workers today. A resilient and thoughtful theology and spirituality as well as innovative skills and frameworks are needed if faithful, effective and sustainable responses are to be found.

God is Creator and sustainer of all, including cities. While we aspire to see our cities more resilient, sustainable and fully humane, we recognize that human hubris, trying to live as if God doesn't matter and unseen forces can be an impediment to these good intentions. We went to Habitat III to learn from others at the conference and to discuss and share our view on cities from a gospel perspective. We found areas of common cause, some areas of difference, but most of all we prayed to find ways to be of loving service helping to build communities in cities, towns, villages, and neighborhoods that embody God's desire for shalom, work which of course will be consummated when Christ returns. This volume is an attempt to distill ways in which faith communities can make a difference.

Cities are contexts that morph and move with unseen powers. No one is immune from these powers and their influence. Christians are no exception. How we identify these powers, their visions and their arenas of play is crucial if Christians are to make a real contribution to the city.

Some key arenas can be identified where battles for the soul of the city are played out. These arenas effect the lives of all people in the city. Areas like politics, education, environment, design, worldview, cultures, media all come together with diverse visions and powers, impacting the city's future. For many Christians, these are simply 'secular' parts of society and outside the scope of what the Church's mission. Even if individual Christians have concerns for such matters, the coming together as 'church' as organization quickly squeezes out time and space to seriously enter these arenas. So often immediate concerns in churches like the seating, parking, singing, preaching and programing take over and consume attention. We call for a fresh centering on God as Source of All Life.

There is a need for a fresh conversion to 'Jesus as Center of Life' that requires us to engage Jesus as a risen, living person and to see him through the lives of the poor, in community as well as the spaces we inhabit in profound ways. Nothing is outside the concerns of Jesus, especially those spheres that affect lives. A key text for us is Colossians 1:16-18;

> *For in him all things in heaven and on earth were created, things visible and invisible, whether thrones or dominions or rulers or powers—all things have been created through him and for him. He himself is before all things, and in him all things hold together. He is the head of the body, the church; he is the beginning, the firstborn from the dead, so that he might come to have first place in everything.*

A Christian approach to transforming urban people and places must include showing up to engage the arenas that impact the future of the city Christians live in. If God is present in 'all things' and Jesus rose from the dead to defeat all powers that would impede a city flourishing, then we can have real hope for shalom to come.

We Need a Fresh Vision of God's Urban Shalom.

In Quito, we also recognized that our vision for our cities has not always been God's vision. We have too often become pre-occupied with our own churches and organizations and have ignored what God wants to do in the people and places we inhabit. There is a mystery here that we often miss, not taking the time to discern what God is doing amongst us and joining him in it.

However, there is hope, one of the things I've enjoyed about editing this book is seeing the depth and breadth of involvement that many people of faith already have with the city from place making to urban planning, mentoring young people to working in some of the most impoverished neighborhoods in the world. There is an opportunity here to move out of our church silo and encourage others to move out of their organizational or institutional silos and begin to think through a shalom or human flourishing framework that allows us to embrace more holistic solutions to systemic issues in cities. Our urban spaces and places will only reach their potential as we all bring what we have been gifted with to the task of creating shalom.

Our effort through this volume is to unpack the city and more of what we mean by shalom; explore issues of discipleship; disparity; diversity and design. The first section will help us shape a theology of the city. The second, focuses on application exploring the creation of shalom with young people as a focus, what it means to build great communities and the importance of land rights.

In chapter one, I'll attempt to unpack the context of a city, the effect of globalization and paint a broad framework for the application of shalom in the urban environment. Ash Barker a well known activist, speaker and writer, who with his family lived in Klong Toey, the largest slum in Bangkok, for 12 years, will continue, focusing on the need for us to be continually converted toward Jesus, community and the poor. He provides some very practical tools and insights for this journey.

Likewise, Evelyn Miranda-Feliciano's work uses biblical reflection to paint a very clear picture of both the disparity present in our modern cities and the cries of the poor for justice, which we must hear. Now deceased, Evelyn was not present at Quito yet her writing is a prophetic voice which comes with years of experience living and working in the Asian context. Hers is an important voice to heed as Asia is home to many of the world's emerging mega-cities.

Michael Mata is director of Transformational Urban Leadership at Azusa-Pacific Seminary and has been involved in community and church based urban transformation for more than 30 years. In his chapter, he reflects on the challenges and importance of cultural diversity. Michael takes us on a journey around the global village, helping us to realize that diversity is all around, and that we can embrace it as part of God's shalom because of our ethic of hospitality and our desire to see Christ in the face of the other.

In our rapidly growing cities, urban design that creates open spaces of welcome is becoming more and more important. Chris Miller, Professor in design at Judson University explores the role urban planning can take in creating neighborhoods that reflect shalom. He shows that the way we experiment with design in our neighborhoods can bring justice and beauty.

Bryan McCabe is a pastor, professor of urban missiology at Bakke Graduate University and heads up the LAMP mentoring initiative. His chapter on the empowerment of young people and the role they can play in creating shalom in their neighborhoods is a helpful guide offering clarifying perspective and practical tools to engage urban youth in transformation.

Long-time community activist, Mary Nelson shares a perspective on the urban poor that can only come from years of living and working towards neighborhood transformation. She encourages us to see that everyone has a gift to bring to the planning table, particularly those we often overlook.

Her very practical story based chapter on seeing people and communities with new eyes brings the New Urban Agenda into the neighborhood and provides tools for us to join with the poor in renewing our communities.

Our last chapter shows that the basis of economic renewal, according to Viv Grigg is land ownership. Viv's chapter on the importance of land rights for the urban poor is only one outcome from over 40 years of living and working in some of the most difficult communities in the world. He writes from the perspective of an urban practitioner passionate about seeing God's justice for the poor. His call is for us to join their struggle.

We recognize there are many gaps in this book, most notably the voice of the majority world. Urban Shalom Publishing which is publishing this title also has a journal *The New Urban World,* in which we aim to continue this conversation from a global perspective.

I hope and pray you find your journey through these chapters as inspiring as I did. More so I hope you hear echoes of your own journey and the response God is calling you to make. I pray that you will join with countless others around the world to play your part in creating cities of shalom.

Andre Van Eymeren
Lead Editor

Section 1

Theology and Thinking About the City

Creating Shalom in the City: A Roadmap for Human Flourishing

1

Andre Van Eymeren

In Christian circles, there is a growing movement of people that recognize the importance of cities, and the part they can play in enhancing every person's experience of shalom. The reality is that half of the world's population lives in a city. That's 3.5 billion people, this figure is expected to rise to 60% by 2030! As a community of faith, the city is a cultural phenomenon that we need to engage with, after all its shalom is our shalom. Generally, despite many references to cities throughout the bible, we have been slow to recognize and value the city as a way that God uses to organize the world and its peoples. We have tended to see cities in a neutral or negative light; as places where people often live in overcrowded conditions, experience poverty and the numerous issues associated with lack of resources, relationships or voice, where there is exploitation, mistrust and miscommunication, or where decisions are made by those exercising power with very little consultation with those at the grassroots or margins who are affected by those decisions. Generally, in the Christian world we have not sought to engage with cities, or if we have, it's been with a somewhat narrow evangelistic, salvation focused approach, which has largely not effected things like city development, social infrastructure, land use, the environment, policy frameworks, place making, poverty and so on. With the global conversation shifting to focus on cities, together with the work being done towards the New Urban Agenda it is a helpful time for the church to re-focus on the city and to partner with others towards the creation of urban shalom, that is spaces and places we can all call home, flourish in and through which reach our potential.

A Brief Landscape of Developing Cities

I don't know about you but cities fascinate me. Have you ever been in a plane flying into a new city? You're sitting in the aisle seat, coming into land and you find yourself straining over 2 people to see out the tiny gap that is the plane's window. If you are anything like me, you're hoping to catch a glimpse of a new city, the buildings on the horizon or the shape of the freeways below, the cars, factories, rows of houses all looking miniature, yet each representing a unique story of individuals in the midst of their daily lives. I can imagine them moving in and out of community, relationship and fundamentally yet almost imperceptibly being influenced by the city around them. Or maybe you've experienced that feeling when you are about to explore a new city (and you can get past the fear of getting lost), everything looking so shiny and new, exciting potentials on every corner. The traveller certainly has a unique perspective to offer the city.

I live in Melbourne, Australia, frequently referred to as the world's most liveable city. I'm not entirely sure what that means, however I am profoundly grateful every time I take long enough to peer out from my balcony on the seventh floor and see the sun glinting in the windows of the buildings opposite or look down the street and see it coming to life in the morning light, the cafes opening, familiar strangers greeting each other at the tram stop and the smell of coffee and fresh baked goods filling the air.

However, the shiny city is not everyone's experience. For some the city is filled with smashed hopes and broken dreams and a monotony of poverty and mindless work that can leave one numb to the beauty surrounding them.

According to the 2015 final report on the Millennium Development Goals, (Millennium Goals, 2015), whilst there has been a significant reduction in globalized poverty, extreme poverty still affects 14% of the developed world (836 Million people) with those people living on less than $1.25 a day. A further half of the workforce in developing regions earns less than what they need to survive. Big gaps still exist between rich and poor households, with children from the poorest 20% twice as likely to be stunted in their growth and not reach the age of five.

As stated by a 2014 report issued by the Oxford Poverty and Human Development Initiative (OPHI, 2014) the type of poverty or deprivation differs by location. Rural multi-dimensional poverty (MDP) tends to consist of deprivation of elements such as electricity, water and flooring, whilst those living in MDP in urban settings experience higher child mortality, malnutrition and lower school attendance. In addition, like people living in extreme poverty in rural communities, those in cities have limited access to employment opportunities and income, inadequate and insecure housing, minimal social protection and limited access to adequate health services (The World Bank, 2016). Whilst cities may promise more opportunities for those experiencing extreme poverty (<$1.25/day), this economic indicator may not tell the true story of urban poverty. As populations shift from being rural to urban, there has been a growth in the number of people living in slums (600million). Added to this, the higher cost of living in cities reflects the need to review the economic poverty line, echoing that at least for urban environments extreme poverty may in fact be experienced by those earning $10 or even $20 a day (Dario, 2015).

Whilst only a portion of the 8 millennial development goals specifically address cities, they have been a core context of development over the last 15-20 years. Cities have both helped to alleviate and been the cause of poverty. In addition, the City Summit, hosted in Istanbul in 1996 set an urban agenda that was reviewed as part of the Habitat 3 process culminating in the Quito meetings, held in October 2016.

The work done in Istanbul recognized the complexity of human settlements and sought to provide a holistic framework for their development. Encouragingly, the agenda had a vision of people working together towards a world *where everyone can live in a safe home with the promise of a decent life of dignity, good health, safety, happiness and hope* (United Nations, 2001). This involved recognizing a systemic approach to cities that included encapsulating a political, economic, environmental, ethical and spiritual vision of the city (United Nations, 1996). This vision would be built on the principles of equality, solidarity, partnership, human dignity, respect and co-operation. I'm not sure about you but I can hear a conflict between these ideals and the reality of the neo-liberal, market-driven society that many of us reside in and subtly contribute to.

One of the many agreements made at the Istanbul City Summit was a promise to commit to sustainable patterns of production, consumption, transportation and (human) settlement development. There was also recognition of the need for pollution prevention and the importance of acknowledging the carrying capacity of ecosystems (United Nations, 1996).

Examining the above we can see, so much of the impetus needed and the elements necessary for human flourishing has already been named and affirmed by, political leaders at all levels, academics and members of civil society. However, the evidence is clear, for the most part cities are not yet places that in their very essence promote human flourishing.

One of the core issues preventing human flourishing is the continuing silo approach to city development. In my work as a consultant and researcher into community development I am often astounded by the lack of communication, not only between different drivers or mechanisms within a city but within organizations. I work with a number of local authorities on creative solutions to systemic issues and quite often hear the lament, 'if only planning could see it this way' or questions like 'how do we help our whole organization take on strength based approaches to their work?' A further issue in development is that the means can become the goal, whereas effective development holds at its core a vision of humanity, of what living well as a human means.

Understanding the constituent parts of a city or society is an important first step on a holistic person-centred journey of development. Dr David Wilson through his work with Sophia Think Tank listed ten drivers of the city; politics, health, education, sport and recreation, business, community service organizations (not for profit), media, arts, Justice and Law (Wilson, 2011). Whilst others might divide a city differently, it's useful to visualize the parts of the whole and then work to bring representation from each of these areas to the table for what is known as synergistic or 'working together' dialogue. The aim of such dialogue is to design solutions to development blocks from an all-in or holistic perspective as opposed to siloed approaches that seem to exacerbate the issue.

However even these dialogues can fall short of helpful development if we fail to have a solid picture of what human flourishing looks like and the elements that make it possible. Viewing the development of our cities through the lens of shalom can help provide a robust roadmap.

What is shalom and how can we en-flesh it?

I recently had the privilege of spending a week away on a writing retreat in Ohio. Among the participants were a group of rabbis. I appreciated being able to sit with them and explore the commonalities of our faith. I had this paper and other research I am conducting into shalom and cities in the back of my mind and asked them whether I could test my understanding of the concept of shalom. One of the ways I explained it was the *wellbeing of the individual in the context of their community*. The rabbis agreed.

The Hebrew understanding of the world is more holistic or inclusive than ours and doesn't draw the distinctions that we might between individual and community, work and the rest of life or even the divisions we create within our own being. Likewise, the concept of shalom even when used as a greeting encompasses everything necessary for healthful living. This includes good physical and emotional health, a sense of wellbeing, good fortune, cohesiveness of the community, relationship to relatives and their state of being and everything else deemed necessary for everything to be in order (Westermann, 1992).

Straight away from this definition we understand shalom to be more than individual peace or even peace between people or nations. The idea of shalom equating to peace did however become a core focus. Many of the debates around the nature of shalom took place in the late 1960's and early 1970's when peace was seen as the absence of war. This became problematic for defining shalom as it was quickly interpreted as peace, with the contemporary idiom being played back on the biblical text. Westermann argues that through a proper understanding of the context of Old Testament usage, shalom can never be the opposite of war, as it is possible to ask about the shalom of the war, meaning the wellbeing of the soldiers. Rather, shalom needs to be seen as completeness, wholeness or wellbeing in the present. This is helpful for our purposes as we explore the development of cities, recognizing that they can be sick just like a person and that wholeness will be different in different situations.

The Scriptures provide us with some windows into the nature, principles and features of shalom, allowing us to apply them directly to the development of cities. Isaiah 65:17-25 is a helpful passage in this regard. Imagine living in a city where the old and young are valued for who they are and they have a clear avenue for contributing to the whole of society.

This city is also a place where people's basic needs for food and shelter are met. Not by handouts but by enabling people to meet these needs for themselves, thus creating a healthy reciprocity. People are also engaged in meaningful work, where work is related to personhood, dignity and the ability to meet needs, not mindless labour for disconnected corporate entities. The city also regularly celebrates its life in ways that are inclusive and promotes wellbeing. The city guided by shalom also experiences harmony between different ethnic groups, people of varying socio-economic standing and those with different levels of education.

Isaiah sees that all these things are undergirded by a relationship with God. Whilst I affirm this idea and recognize that God is the originator of shalom, it is possible to move towards developing a city like this by partnering with others who may not necessarily own our Christian faith but in fact desire a very similar world. Flipping this idea we may in fact find God through the creation of this sort of environment. After all where the values of God's Kingdom are present, isn't that where the Kingdom is?

Jeremiah demonstrates this clearly in his letter to the exiles (chapter 29). He encourages the Jewish people to build houses, settle down, eat the fruit of their gardens, have families and seek the prosperity of the city. In other words, work towards the common good, because as they do this, the people themselves will also prosper or experience shalom. Durham points out that there is room for a secular understanding of shalom (Durham, 1992) and it is clear that God has no intentions of withholding his blessing from Babylon. When we seek to partner with others outside the church we may have to change our language using terms such as wellbeing, harmony, common good, justice and so forth but they are synonymous with or at least describe aspects of the full picture of shalom.

Whilst shalom can tend to focus on the family or small community this can easily be enlarged. Westermann gives the example of a stranger arriving in town, he waits in the city square for someone to take him in. He is given the greeting 'peace be with you,' and naturally following on from this greeting the stranger is invited into the enquirer's home and is given food, drink, and feed for his donkey. In this way, shalom takes on a universal flavour, by the family or clan accepting the stranger into their circle of shalom, they are giving the circle unrestricted breadth (Westermann, 1992). Perhaps our equivalent is living the big or kenotic life, particularly at this time with issues such as rising homelessness, increased political polarity, institutional cruelty towards asylum seekers, a general state-sanctioned meanness of spirit and the numerous concerns around poverty in developing cities. An attitude akin to the ancient Hebrew approach to hospitality may well be the foundation of a shalom fuelled remedy to some of the big issues we face in developing cities around the world.

In this sense, shalom relates to justice. Themes of Justice are of course echoed throughout the Scriptures but are particularly prevalent in Amos and Micah, where the call to let justice flow like a river and the connection between loving justice and walking humbly with God are made. Justice and the concept of a whole of society shalom is picked up by Jesus in his manifesto in Luke 4:18 where he cries for the freedom of the oppressed, restoration of sight to the blind and the proclamation of good news to the poor. NT Wright points out the good news is in fact that the world can be different now, the marginalized do not have to stay in the background, the quality of the redeemed life and indeed a redeemed world can at least in part be experienced in the present (Wright, 2008). In Matthew 5, commonly known as the beatitudes, Jesus invites us to join with him in fashioning an inner attitude and outward actions that can bring about this new order in the here and now.

The establishing of shalom highlights an enduring partnership between God and man. This is illustrated well in the story of Israel wanting a king (1 Sam 8:20). God graciously allows this to happen, but sets a very clear mandate for the king. He is to, with God ensure the stability of the world as a place to live and where crops and herd animals are fertile. He is to work towards the absence of war, as well as social justice and the wellbeing of marginalized communities (Steck, cited in Duchrow & Liedke, 1987). It sounds simple but what would it mean for governments today to partner with other spheres of society including churches, towards these goals?

Brueggemann elaborates about the nature of shalom in this context. He understands that every creature is in community with every other, living in harmony toward the joy and wellbeing of every other creature. And that essentially all people are the children of one family and heirs of a single hope (Breuggemann, 1976). This allows us to dream with God, of the human family working together towards the common good. The concept that shalom can be experienced in civil society is both confronting and exciting. Confronting as it can push us out of our Christianized bubbles and help us realize that God's dream for the world encompasses all of it and is not limited to a selected few who sit on the margins, watching the rest of humanity and the created order spiral more and more out of control. Once we have come to terms with this reality, we are then compelled to take God's desires seriously, which will open the doors for partnership with the city.

What could our cities look like?

> *Never doubt that a small group of thoughtful, committed citizens can change the world; indeed, it's the only thing that ever has.*
> Margaret Mead

Working with God on designing the city in the way he longs for, starts with a hope based, people centred dream rather than pragmatics. Understandably so much of development writing and action focuses on infrastructure, education, eliminating extreme poverty, good health and wellbeing, climate action, gender equality, responsible consumption, economic growth, sustainable cities and communities and justice. These are important foci in fact they describe the essence of the 17 sustainable development goals that will set the development agenda until 2030 (United Nations, 2016). Whilst each of the goals will benefit people living in some of the poorest communities in the world and hopefully positively affect the planet, together they lack a vision of what it means to flourish. Put another way we need to enact an enriched sustainability. This is the unique contribution or point of difference to use marketing language that people of faith can contribute. This fact does not put us at the lead of the conversation or above other contributions, but simply provides us with an entry point into the debate towards the common good and allows us to genuinely partner with others towards God's objectives.

The New Urban Agenda (United Nations, 2016) recognizes that whilst there have been significant steps forward in alleviating extreme poverty and creating healthy cities, the job is not complete. *However, the persistence of multiple forms of poverty, growing inequalities, and environmental degradation, remain the major obstacles to sustainable development worldwide, with social and economic exclusion and spatial segregation often an irrefutable reality in cities and human settlements.*

Even with its own set of challenges, the New Urban Agenda highlights urbanisation as an opportunity and engine room to propel us towards sustainable development. It advocates for a readdressing of the way cities and human settlements are planned, financed and governed. Encouragingly the first point of its vision emphasizes the concept of cities for all. Recognizing that everyone has the right to equal use and enjoyment of the city.

> ...seeking to promote inclusivity and ensure that all inhabitants, of present and future generations, without discrimination of any kind, are able to inhabit and produce just, safe, healthy, accessible, resilient, and sustainable cities and human settlements, as a common good that essentially contributes to prosperity and quality of life (United Nations, 2016).

The last sentence is of particular interest and provides a useful entry point for people of faith. Whilst many of us will have professional contribution to make at any number of levels on the development and implementation of national and local policies, the call to a people-centred approach to cities rings true to the biblical narrative, giving us a sustained voice in any city development focused conversation.

The Genesis creation story clearly puts human beings in the centre of God's story. We are created to be image bearers and as such have the capacity for self-giving love, creativity, beauty, justice, compassion, wisdom as well as a need for and the capacity to draw strength from stillness, purpose, belonging and community. We see these traits of God throughout the biblical narrative both in the divine and when humanity is at its best. When embraced they lead to human flourishing. There is no clearer example of them than in the person of Jesus, who modelled a way of living that, in the context of Middle Eastern society demonstrated to us the principles of the full life. Through his death and resurrection, he made it clear that the qualities he modelled are in fact meant for life now and that they will be fulfilled when finally, the realm of heaven where God is in complete control comes to earth. In the meantime, enabled by the presence of the divine in the world (not just Christians) through the Holy Spirit we are to partner with him and others of like mind to begin work on what will be our ultimate glorious (God honoring) reality.

Aligning with the Sustainable Development Goals and a host of other development focused declarations, the New Urban Agenda has an 8-point vision for what cities could be. It includes;

- The fulfilling of the cities social function as a part of the right to an adequate standard of living.
- The promotion of civic engagement as well as a sense of belonging and ownership, providing a context for social cohesion and the meeting of needs.
- Gender equality and the full and effective participation and equal rights in all fields including leadership and decision-making.
- Sustainable economic growth, seeing urbanisation as a vehicle for structural transformation, high productivity, value added activities, resource efficiency and the harnessing of local economies.

- Seeing cities as hubs and drivers for balanced, sustainable and integrated urban and territorial or regional development.
- Effective urban mobility, linking people, places, goods, services and economic opportunities.
- Disaster risk reduction, reducing vulnerability and building resilience and responsiveness to natural and man-made hazards.

The creation of sustainable consumption and production patterns and protection or restoration of ecosystems and biodiversity. (United Nations, 2016)

For so long in the church we have ignored the expertise that God has put in our midst. Within any congregation, but particularly the church across a city there is a representation of nearly every profession or job type, each person with a contribution to make. As was the prophet's call to the Jews in exile in Babylon we are to work for the benefit, shalom, flourishing, prosperity of the city for if it is doing well, then the shalom of all people and that city will be increased. Thinking of our mission in this way reduces the unhelpful dichotomy between God's Kingdom and this world, the spiritual and material and breaks down that horrible 'us and them' attitude that can so easily seep into our approach to the world.

The Role of the Church

There have been many books written on the role of the church in the world, there is not the space here to debate the various approaches and what those approaches say about our soteriology and eschatology. We believe the church's mission is to partner with God in the creation of a world that reflects his dream for the coming Kingdom. It is God's mission, not ours and so a vital part of our responsibility to the world is to continue to seek his design. This will involve a central connection to Jesus and through him a diligent study of the Word and the ability to apply it in a very different world to the one in which it was written. With this commitment comes a call to a deep spirituality that moves us beyond the Sunday service to a life of discipleship, where we are caught up in God's heart and find ourselves in the midst of his plan for the world.

This enables us to have a generous attitude to the world, where we look for God's presence, rather than only lament his absence. As we do this we are more open to receive the other and the contribution they have which joins with ours towards a better world. Through these understandings, the church is able to model a life of shalom, and engage in advocacy and partnership towards its creation.

Acts 2:44-47 clearly shows a community that is attempting to live out a vision of shalom in the world. Having lived in some form of intentional Christian community for the most part of the last 20 years it is not easy or very natural to share possessions, create a common life and then live a shared witness, however it is within the very struggle to live out the reality of a full life that we meet God. In the meeting of God in this way I became painfully aware of my need for continued transformation. Pointing in turn to the need for ongoing discipleship in the context of a community or environment that can continue to challenge us to become more and more our authentic self. As together we go on this journey, almost by accident it creates an alternative approach to the world, one that is counter cultural yet to the seeker or fellow sojourner a community that is incredibly enticing.

A community base gives us a platform from which to advocate and partner with other people of peace towards the picture of the world we all share. I've spent much of my ministry living and working in socioeconomically depressed communities. One such community is Dandenong in the South East of Melbourne. It is one of Australia's most multicultural communities with people coming from over 150 different birthplaces. Its weekly median income is around $400, $200 less than the Melbourne average. Most employment is in the manufacturing industry, with unemployment around 3% more than the Melbourne average (City of Greater Dandenong, 2016). By world standards, not extreme poverty, however families and individuals have been caught in the generational poverty trap creating significant tensions with the push for gentrification in the community.

Due to this push and many other factors such as housing affordability, poor mental health, drug and alcohol abuse, unemployment, relationship breakdown and the list goes on, more and more people are finding themselves living in rooming houses or even caravan parks. Shawlands is one of those caravan parks. When I was first introduced to the park, it was dirty, overgrown, the vans were run down and the police were on hand sometimes up to 3 times a day. Transformation happened through 2 coinciding events. A new owner took over the park and the Dandenong Reformed Church began work in the community. One of the church's first tasks was to create a network of all the social services and local government associated with the park (that became my role). As this network formed the church developed significant on the ground partnerships with other agencies that also wanted to improve the lives of those living in the park. A core difference between the church and the other agencies was the focus on relationships and the transformative power of creating a community of belonging. After a time, it became a broker of relationship for and with the other agencies.

The network also became a place of advocacy, where the needs of those in the park and eventually beyond, to include boarding houses were highlighted to the services and the local council. This is an on-going network that continues to benefit the lives of some of the most vulnerable in the community. All over the world there are similar stories of the church partnering with local officials and services towards the common good. Often in these instances the motivation for engagement and partnership cannot be well articulated, but there is a sense of its rightness. However, without a clear theology of engagement, it is all too easy to lose focus and divert energy inwards particularly when a crisis of some sort hits. The more positive alternative is to let a well understood motivation for mission or engagement be the core defining influence of the church, giving rise to an inner expression that supports the mission.

Conclusion

As a landscape for mission, the city is rich, containing both excruciating need and unparalleled opportunity. As people of faith, we are in a unique position to partner with others bringing our understanding of what it means to flourish and live life from the perspective of shalom. In the last 15-20 years cities have been a core platform for development, with over half the world's population residing in an urban environment. Despite the drop in extreme poverty and rise in global education and other positive developments, cities remain places where many are marginalized, feeling like they don't belong or where people are trapped in mindless poverty cycles they perceive will never end.

Into this milieu we have the opportunity to introduce the concept of shalom a hope-based, people-centred concept that encapsulates whole of life wellbeing. Shalom asks about the wellbeing of the individual in the context of community. Much of what we read in passages such as Isaiah 65:17-25 resonates with the type of life others are striving for, setting up the opportunity for robust partnerships toward the creation of the world that God dreams of. Into the partnership, we bring a picture of what it means to flourish both individually and communally. This picture is based on the fact that we, along with all of humanity are image bearers of God and living life to the full means reflecting that image into the world.

As people of faith we can reflect this image through modelling the type of community that will lead to flourishing as well as advocating for and working towards change. To see this become a reality we need to partner with others on a whole range of projects that work toward a city where the young and old are valued and have a way to contribute, where people are enjoying meaningful work and the fruit of that work and where there is an openness to embrace and celebrate with the other. A city characterized by shalom.

References

Brueggemann, W. (1976). *Living Towards A Vision: Biblical Reflections on Shalom.* Philadelphia: United Church Press.

City of Greater Dandenong. (2016). *Social Statistics.* Retrieved on 12 August, 2016, from http://www.greaterdandenong.com/document/42/social-statistics

Duchrow, U. & Liedke, G. (1987). *Shalom: Biblical Perspectives on Creation, Justice and Peace.* Geneva: WCC Publications.

Dario, B. (2015, November 24). Urban Poverty and Slums: The future of poverty is now. (weblog post). Retrieved from http://www.poverties.org/blog/urban-poverty

Habitat 3. (2016). Habitat III: Draft New Urban Agenda, 28 July 2016. Retrieved on 12 August, 2016, from http://habitat3.org/wp-content/uploads/Surabaya-Draft-New-Urban-Agenda-28-July-2016.

Oxford Poverty & Human Development Initiative. (2014). *Poverty in Rural and Urban Areas: Direct comparisons using the global MPI 2014.* Retrieved August 10, 2016, from http://www.ophi.org.uk/wp-content/uploads/Poverty-in-Rural-and-Urban-Areas-Direct-Comparisons-using-the-Global-MPI-2014.pdf.

The World Bank. (2016). *Urban Poverty: An Overview.* Retrieved August 10, 2016, from http://go.worldbank.org/19N9ZIG9K0

United Nations. (2015). *The Millennium Development Goals Report 2015.* Retrieved August 9, 2016, from http://www.un.org/millenniumgoals/2015_MDG_Report/pdf/MDG%202015%20rev%20(July%201).pdf.

United Nations. (2001). *The Habitat Agenda: Istanbul Declaration on Human Settlement.* Retrieved August 11, 2016, from http://www.un.org/ga/Istanbul+5/declaration.htm.

United Nations. (1996). *The Habitat Agenda: Chapter II: Goals and Principles.* Retrieved August 11, 2016 from http://www.un-documents.net/ha-2.htm)

United Nations. (2016). *Sustainable Development Goals.* Retrieved on 12 August, 2016, from http://www.un.org/sustainabledevelopment/sustainable-development-goals/

Westermann, C. (1992). Peace (Shalom) in the Old Testament. In P. Yoder and Swartley (Eds). *The Meaning of Peace*. Louisville, Institute of Mennonite Studies.

Wilson, D. (2011). *Ten Drivers of Society.* Retrieved November 2, 2015, from https://biblevic.wordpress.com/ten-drivers-of-society/

Wright, T. (2007). *Surprised By Hope*. London: SPCK.

Urban Shalom & Conversions to Discipleship

2

Ash Barker

The world has been rapidly changing and is challenging the very nature of Christian faith and mission as we know it. A fundamental change with significant implications for Christians is how and where humans live together. In 1800 only 3% of people lived in cities, but now more than half of all humans live in urban areas with over one third facing severe urban poverty. With over 70% of people predicted to be urbanites by 2050, the increased disparity, diversity and density of living will leave no person, place or culture untouched.

Areas of urban deprivation and poverty are especially complex places to make a long-term impact, but they are some of the most critical frontline contexts for mission today. A resilient and thoughtful theology and spirituality as well as innovative skills and frameworks are needed if effective, sustainable responses are to be found.

In this chapter, we will explore the nature and call of Christian discipleship as a core motif in response to these growing urban realities. Understanding the context in which we find ourselves is crucial however, this chapter will focus on the significance of various conversions that help centre us on the risen Jesus. These conversions empower us to engage with his concerns as a way of faithful commitment from within these contexts. A core question becomes how can Christian discipleship inform and inspire our spirituality, practices and vision for our new urban world?

The need for multiple conversions

Che Guevara wasn't always an icon for revolutions and activists. He was a middle, upper class medical student before he took an adventure with a friend on a motor-bike around Bolivia. The movie "The Motorcycle Diaries" follows this road trip, and like many such films, a dramatic conversion point is experienced in a key scene that would alter the trajectory of Che's life forever. In the movie Che celebrates his birthday with staff at the leper colony where he had volunteered as a doctor. They were on one side of the river, while the lepers were on the other side. In the dark, and against the anguished protests of friends and colleagues Che risks the currents, crocodiles and struggling with asthma dives into the water to swim to the other side. As his breathing becomes more strained it's not clear if he will make it. As Che gets closer to the other side his patients with leprosy hear the noise and they gather on the bank to cheer him on. As Che rises out of the water exhausted the Lepers meet and embrace him. Che's allegiances and priorities were transformed forever. He was on a different side of the river now both physically and metaphorically.

It's a funny, but powerful scene. Whatever we make of Che's politics, this scene reminds me that faith is an adventure and requires life altering conversions too. If Christians are to fully invest in God's coming urban Shalom - cities living as Jesus intends - then life with Jesus should enable us to live in radically different ways than if we hadn't met Jesus and started living for shalom. As in the movie, our adventures with Jesus should mean we can't stay on the safe side of the river and simply provide a safe service. God's Compassion once embraced calls us to overcome barriers and become different people. These conversions can't be forced or worked up by hype or guilt, but they can come as embrace, encounter and new engagement and insight on the discipleship journey. Like Che Guevara's conversion as he crossed over to be with lepers and become a revolutionary, so should our lives be different for meeting Jesus and investing ourselves in the coming urban shalom.

Zacchaeus had such conversions with Jesus. As recorded in Luke's Gospel Jesus says of Zacchaeus "salvation has come to this house today, for this man also is a descendant of Abraham." He had experienced a conversion in a popular Christian understanding of conversion. Yet, as we read more carefully we see the deeper nature of Christian conversions. If we join Jesus in seeking first the Kingdom in our cities what will it mean for us?

Please take some time to prayerfully read Luke 19:1-10. What conversions do you see here?

> He [Jesus] entered Jericho and was passing through it. A man was there named Zacchaeus; he was a chief tax-collector and was rich. He was trying to see who Jesus was, but on account of the crowd he could not, because he was short in stature. So he ran ahead and climbed a sycamore tree to see him, because he was going to pass that way. When Jesus came to the place, he looked up and said to him, 'Zacchaeus, hurry and come down; for I must stay at your house today.' So, he hurried down and was happy to welcome him. All who saw it began to grumble and said, 'He has gone to be the guest of one who is a sinner.' Zacchaeus stood there and said to the Lord, 'Look, half of my possessions, Lord, I will give to the poor; and if I have defrauded anyone of anything, I will pay back four times as much.' Then Jesus said to him, 'Today salvation has come to this house, because he too is a son of Abraham. For the Son of Man came to seek out and to save the lost.'

What was Zacchaeus like before he met Jesus?

Luke is often careful to show us the difference Jesus makes. This can especially be seen in who Zacchaeus is before he met Jesus in the urban area of Jericho. Set in this place where Priests and Levites lived and rested between service at the Temple in Jerusalem, and where Jewish nationalism was strong. Zacchaeus' identity, allegiances and his vulnerabilities would be known by Luke's first readers as his conversion unfolds. Here are some of the most obvious starting points for Zacchaeus.

First, Zacchaeus was a person with *power*. As a "man" who was the "Chief tax collector" in first century Palestine he had sided with the invading Roman Empire against his own oppressed people. As a tool of the Roman machine, the life and death of those around him was in his hands. He represented the might of Rome as he did his work for them. As the story unfolds it is clear Zacchaeus abused this power and was corrupt even by the standards of Roman law and order. Today Colonizers may not have the power they once did, but the concentration of wealth among the few elites and the need for others to do their bidding is still part of how Global Empires do business. We may not have Rome, but there are still Empires that concentrate power and both give and take it away. Zacchaeus was one who sided with the Empire.

This passed on power made Zacchaeus *rich*. To be sure, the description of "wealthy" is a relative term. In first Century Palestine he would not have had access to electricity, running water or mobile phones as many today would have and still be described as "poor" in comparison to the average. He would, however, have had the trappings of power and status compared to others. More importantly he had the economic freedom to decide how he lived and still have surplus. Even today wealth and poverty is more about the ability to make decisions about our own lives and those around us with whom we are in relationship with than mere cash. Zacchaeus was, according to the text, 'rich'.

Zacchaeus was *isolated*. There was a cost to this power and wealth. He is described as "small", "ran ahead of the crowd", "climbed up a tree" all by himself. In the context of nationalistic Jericho he was especially vulnerable to his fellow Jews. It would have been a surprise to all that Jesus would want to relate with him and receive his hospitality. Despite his power and wealth, a loneliness and lack of loving connections with others seems to have dehumanized him. This alienation from others and abuse of others, is, perhaps, a defining characteristic of so many lives in cities today. Used and being used creates deep fear and loneliness. All this makes Zacchaeus seem smaller and literally stuck up a tree by himself.

He was also a *spectator*. He was away from the action on the ground, just waiting to "see Jesus go past". This lack of personal engagement and stake in the unfolding history going past makes Zachueas seem like a tragic figure. He is a pawn not really a player after all, but he can view the action safely from a vantage point. Like so many in cities today he is content to watch from a safe distance, avoiding personal cost or trauma. Any connection with the drama of change is viewed vicariously, not personally. Today this impulse to simply watch anonymously, to be entertained and not participate is perhaps a characteristic urban temptation. Zacchaeus was content to watch Life pass him by.

If ever there was a biblical character that embodied the challenges of so many urban people today, including many who describe themselves as Christian, it's Zacchaeus. His characteristics of being *powerful, wealthy,* and an *isolated spectator* in the divine drama rings true in cities all over the world. Cities today are magnifying these qualities and their impact is being felt on the whole Earth.

As this Gospel story unfolds, we find that with Jesus it doesn't have to be this way for Zacchaeus or for us in our urban environments. We can be converted and keep being converted like Zacchaeus. This is Good News in every sense for a world where rapid urbanization has the capacity to fracture, alienate and dehumanize us from each other and our sense of place.

Zacchaeus' Four "Conversions"

I'm using the term 'conversion' quite intentionally here. It's about experiencing a whole-sale change in our life-priorities, allegiances and very identity. As Christians, we believe that this happens as we encounter, follow and join Jesus. I know conversion is a term that has been high-jacked by 'revivalists' as just between God and the individual's heart, but this is not the Gospel meaning of the term '*metatnoia*' the right response to the Good News. Often translated 'repentance', our English word 'metamorphosis' comes from this root word. So it about total ongoing change, growth and transformation.

Unless there is a fundamental conversion in our lives, making us different because we join Jesus, we have not truly been converted to Christ. There is far too much nominalism amongst us who call ourselves Christian. To change the world, to see God's will done on earth as in heaven, to see urban shalom come, we need the four conversions that Zacchaeus had.

Just a quick note on my influences here. The term 'triple conversion of discipleship' is one that was common among Christian radicals years ago. I first heard this term in the 1990s from my late mentor and PhD supervisor Ross Langmead. It struck me then, as now, as helping us evaluate our experiences of joining with Jesus and inviting us to go deeper. I have added a fourth conversion that makes more explicit the environmental and 'place-based' conversion that was often assumed by Ross and others in the 'Radical Discipleship Movement'.

As we reflect together on these four conversions that Zacchaeus and the early disciples experienced in the New Testament I would love you to keep connecting with your own experiences. Can we keep having these conversion experiences with Jesus too? Can we keep inviting others into these encounters?

What are the four conversions for urban shalom?

1. Converted to Jesus

"*Welcomed Jesus with great joy*" (v6)

Jesus found Zacchaeus up in his tree and Zacchaeus was first and foremost converted to the living Jesus of Nazareth. It was Jesus who took the initiative and Zacchaeus responded. What does the text say about what Jesus was like? What was it that caused Zacchaeus to pledge his allegiance to him? Three quick observations about Jesus in this encounter:

First, we can see Jesus was on a revolutionary adventure, turning the world upside down. This adventure came to Zacchaeus' own neighborhood, but it was moving. Jesus was "Passing through Jericho" on his way to "Jerusalem". (Lk 18:31) It was Jesus' adventure to join and not simply Zacchaeus adding Jesus to his life. Jesus is the centre of life and not us.

Second, we can see that Jesus 'looks' for Zacchaeus. A core part of Jesus' vocation was to "seek and save the lost". (v10) Zacchaeus was hiding in a tree, but the eyes of Jesus went beyond his motivations, fear and decisions. Jesus saw the ones that knew they needed to change, for whom the status quoi was not working and found them.

Third, Jesus takes the initiative and invites himself into Zacchaeus' life and home. (v5) Having found Zacchaeus, Jesus enlists him. Zacchaeus is to provide hospitality and in this cultural setting Jesus was therefore in his debt. This was scandalous and shocked the religious leaders, but Jesus insists on empowering those on the edge.

To really encounter this Jesus is so different to modern evangelism and discipleship techniques. Zacchaeus did not make an idol of Jesus in his own image so his life could feel more comfortable. Neither was this discipleship conversion simply a way to get people do join the church and do work or activism for the church, organization or cause. It was certainly not a sentimentalized encounter as if Jesus was a boyfriend to sing to when we feel lonely. No. This Gospel story shows a profound, all of life encounter and conversion to Jesus where home, work, politics and powers are all part of the story. Such a conversion to Jesus requires an ongoing acceptance of him and his invitation for adventures in doing God's will. To keep making the person of the Lord Jesus Christ our first allegiance, "receiving him with great joy" and following him into the revolution still so important for urbanites today. To have a real, personal, immersed encounter with Jesus can change us.

John Wesley was one of the first industrial era evangelists. He saw a movement emerge among urban people who had felt rejected by the Church. A key part of Wesley's understanding was to know the difference between spiritual awakenings and spiritual regeneration. He would preach in fields on the outskirts of towns and cities seeking to help people become awakened to the grace of God in personal encounters with Jesus. It was later, in small group 'class meetings' that those awakened individuals would incubate 'spiritual regeneration'.

We live in an instant society that loves awakening experiences, but hates deep conversions to do another's will in fellowship with others. A tell-tale sign of this conversion or deep allegiance change is how we make decisions. I was once in conversation with a gifted and committed person. I remember them saying, "We'd go anywhere for Jesus, but we need to live near a surf beach. Jesus knows that we love the beach and he knows it keeps us sane. So sorry, there's just no surf in slums or refugee camps." It made perfect sense to them. Of course, I wasn't so easily put off. People used to say, 'God loves you and Ash has a wonderful plan for your life!' So my initial response was to think of slums were surf beaches are, but I could only come up with Banda Acheh where a tsunami had come through.

It struck me then that we can't have pre-conditions, pre-nuptials or 'get out' clauses with Jesus. He is not about magic and trying formulas to get God to give us what we want. Jesus is not about punishing us, trying to make our lives miserable either. Jesus wants us to join him as channels of

God's will and compassion in the world. It cost Jesus his life to do this and it will cost us to be faithful to Jesus in the city. If we surrender all to Jesus, unreservedly, there will be costs but, it is worth anything we give up.

Christian discipleship therefore, is the opposite of cold, mechanistic programs, aimed at socializing people into the church. Far from power abuse, manipulation or brain-washing, the call to Christian discipleship and conversion to Jesus is about finding a new way to live.

Perhaps here it would be helpful to offer a preliminary definition of Christian discipleship that can help us move forward towards discovering what it truly means to be disciples in our new urban world. I have used the following definition, rooted in John 3:16, in various contexts and it has helped find common ground with diverse Christians, but also opens up a dynamic discussion about the nature of Christian faith and mission in urban contexts.

To encounter, follow and join Jesus Christ through the power of the Sprit for the Creator's redeeming agenda in the Cosmos.

Each of the key elements in this short definition need some more attention and can help us engage with key biblical texts, influential scholarship and spiritual exercise around the call to discipleship in cities. Where possible I have tried to find free downloaded resources to aid those who don't have access to full theological libraries. It is worth sitting and praying with some of these classical Christian texts, writings and exercises to deepen your understanding of discipleship and conversion to Jesus.

a) To encounter Jesus

At the heart of the Christian faith is the truth claim that Jesus rose from the dead and can be encountered today. Indeed, the apostle Paul claims that if Jesus did not rise from the dead he was a fool. The experiential nature of Christian faith is a crucial element in discipleship. If we don't at some level meet Jesus personally - beyond the information, ideologies or doctrines *about* Jesus- we miss the Christian faith.

Finding fresh encounters with Jesus within our urban contexts has been a key concern for urban Christian activist-thinkers over the centuries. Here are some recent examples I've found helpful.

E Stanley Jones, an American missionary to cities in India during the turbulent mid-20th century, was a key voice calling for evangelism to focus on encounters with Jesus as a way of 'naturalising Jesus' in any given context. His book 'Christ of the Indian Road' gives examples of how working with local leaders made this possible.[1]

Some more recent activist scholars like Athol Gill in Australia or Ched Myers in the USA became important Gospel scholars, drawing attention to the radical nature of Christian discipleship as it responds 'to the roots' (the basic meaning of the word radical) of our social context with the roots of our faith.[2] This kind of work helps us meet Jesus from the Gospels and not just make up a Jesus that makes us feel good. There is challenging work to do here, but it is crucial that our head, heart and hands encounter the real Jesus.

An Exercise to Try:

Read the whole of Mark's Gospel in one sitting, identifying the various calls to discipleship. What do these calls have in common in terms of encountering Jesus?

b) To follow Jesus

Just meeting Jesus is not enough to see lasting change happen. Indeed, many of the characters who met Jesus in the Gospels did not respond to him positively and left their encounter with Jesus sad.

One of the most influential writers pleading for encounters with Jesus that change allegiances and lifestyle is Dietrich Bonheoffer. His call to resist the dominant forces of the day and be prepared to pay 'the cost of discipleship' by following Jesus was developed deep within the fiery cauldron of Nazi Germany. This call to discipleship did actually cost Bonheoffer his life just days before the end of the Second World War, but his insights and plea continue to influence Christian faith to this day.[3]

An Exercise to Try:

Read and reflect on 'The Rich Young Ruler and Peter' (Luke 18) and imagine what it would have been like if you were in the Rich young rulers place. What was the cost of his 'non-following' of Jesus? How did Peter's response differ from the Rich Young Ruler's?

c) To join Jesus

Globalizing urban contexts can so often create consumers and competitors. To only encounter and try to follow Jesus in our own strength is not enough. We need to fully connect with Jesus as a person and his mission to renew the world. We will discuss more fully later, the nature of community building, but the call to join Jesus so we can be salt and light in the world is a theme taken up by many urban Christian communities and activists. Some of the most influential have been those from Anabaptist movement including Eberhard Arnold's radical call to join Jesus agenda as found in the Sermon on the Mount. Arnold's book *Salt and Light: Living the Sermon on the Mount*[4] inspired the imagination of some of the important names in contemporary theology and spirituality including Barth, Bonhoeffer, Merton and Moltmann. Please read carefully and let it touch your imagination too.

An exercise to try:

Read the Sermon on the Mount (Matthew 5 and 6). In what ways could your life look different if you more fully joined Jesus in living this out?

d) Through the power of the Spirit

The Trinity is a distinctly Christian understanding of God that is crucial to Christian faith and practice. Even as we read such radical works as the above, the temptation to swing from 'cheap grace' to 'law' can occur if there is no power to change coming from outside ourselves. Crippled by guilt and striving ever harder to live an ideal is not the 'abundant life' God intends for urban people and the places they create. So, if deep conversions to Jesus are to occur then it is only possible in the power of the Holy Spirit. If the Spirit comes upon people, then amazing things are possible internally and externally.

One of the most influential contemporary theologians is Jurgen Moltmann. His call to pay attention to radical discipleship in the power of the Spirit inspires and informs like few others.[5] While sometimes difficult to read, his insights have influenced a wide range of Christian thinkers and activists, including Charismatic, Pentecostals, Catholics and mainstream Protestants.

An exercise to try:

Read and reflect on the key text John 14:1-20 which explores the 'The Role of the Holy Spirit". What do you see as the Holy Spirit's role in empowering discipleship?

e) For the Creator's redeeming agenda in the Cosmos

The importance of God as Creator and his plans for the world is also included in this definition of Christian discipleship. Active faith in the God 'who so loved the cosmos' is not just about original creation, but has a future dimension of hope for all creation. The Creator God is redeeming and renewing all creation through Jesus in the power of the Spirit and this includes people and places in the city. It is Jesus' prayer "God's will be done on Earth as in Heaven" that is the agenda of God the Creator.

N.T (Tom) Wright has championed the cause of what has become known as 'realized eschatology' through historical New Testament scholarship. What has begun with the resurrection of Jesus, Wright argues, will be completed when the realms of heaven and earth come together at Jesus' return. This is not about life after death for believers on a distant, disembodied cloud, but God's will and reign being fully present on this Earth as in the Realm of Heaven.[6] As will become apparent how we imagine the Creator God's redemptive plan for the Cosmos matters in what agenda's Christian follow and join.

An exercise to try:

Read and reflect on the key text: 1 Corinthian 15 and the first fruits of Jesus' resurrection. What would the world look life if it was like Jesus' resurrected body?

These key bible passages, scholars and exercises raise many questions as to what is our 'normal, everyday' experience of Christian faith in cities today. Why is there a gap? Have we experienced this conversion to Jesus as person lately ourselves? Do we keep giving Jesus the run of our homes, lives and decisions? How do we prioritize and make decisions?

2. Converted to the Poor

"Listen Jesus, I will give half of my belongings to the poor and if I have cheated any-one I will pay back four times as much" (v8)

Zacchaeus, did not just receive Jesus, he got what Jesus was on about instantly. Jesus is about loving God and neighbors so much that God's kingdom would come on earth as it is in heaven. Zacchaeus therefore, needed to find a way to repent and be in line with this new reign. In Jesus time as now, the biggest barrier to this reign happening is the oppression of poor people. Zacchaeus saw himself in comparison to Jesus as an oppressor and went about repenting to become more like Jesus. Going to the poor and finding restitution then was an important part of joining Jesus in this adventure. If we have power and we follow Jesus he will take us to the margins and the edges.

The importance of those who are pushed to the margins in life is a central concern of Jesus and God's redemptive work. This is true for cities today as much as elsewhere. Yet, even those who want to take Christian discipleship seriously often miss following Jesus to these dark places of suffering.

I must admit poverty is no longer a fashionable word, let alone poor. It seems so labeling, even disparaging of others. Yet, there are around 2,500 verses in Bible that call God's people to engage with 'the poor'. Indeed, it's hard to read any Gospel story where the poor are not somehow involved. Why? Because it is where the systems of this world fail that Jesus' light and life most shines and is needed. This is about being a channel of compassion where it is most needed. If we want to be converted to Jesus then it is crucial to be converted to expressing practical love with those experiencing injustice.

I know so many reading this chapter will have your own stories of this kind of conversion. For so many it is a combination of prayerful Bible reading and getting to really love people facing poverty and the interface of the two in community. Others personally engage those suffering first and then find Jesus there. Whatever the case seeking to change those in need, those that stay and find discipleship, know that Jesus uses the poor to change us. Especially those of us with power and status like Zacchaeus.

I am still haunted by memories of Metakore, but he changed my life. His name meant 'no parent' and we called him Metus as he became one of our first foster sons in my native Melbourne in the early 1990s. When we first met him he was a cute 12-year-old boy with gappy teeth, half-done-up overalls and a smile full of mischief. I can still see him leaning over his pool cue, with concentration engraved in his eyes, trying to impress his huge, teenage Cook Island uncles standing around him. Anji and I were white, educated, middle class and part of a lively church, all of which we thought was "normal". However, God used Metus to open our eyes to see the reality of our social position in relation to those on the margins. Metus loved the youth club we were running. He would often come over to our home and not want to go back to his grandparents. He gradually became part of our family and Anji called him my "shadow".

Metus was not attending school at this time. In fact, he had missed his entire first year of secondary school. So, after talking with his grandparents about him starting his second year at another high school he came to live with us. Metus was not used to any discipline, had a short attention span and could only read very little. We later found out that he also had a mild intellectual disability. But although it was a difficult year for Metus— and his teachers— he did just make it through the whole year. We loved him as a son and considered him part of our family.

Some of my fondest memories of Metus are of him playing soccer and going camping with our youth clubs. He loved rugby and fishing and his chuckling laughter and sense of humour were contagious. On one occasion, while in a boat fishing with us, Metus sneaked off the back of the boat and swam underwater and tried to pull on the other lines so that the other guys fishing thought they had a bite. He especially loved Christmas time and one year dressed up as Santa for all the kids in the street—they had never seen a Santa from the Pacific Islands before. The following year Metus met Denise. She would become his sweetheart and would later have Metus' baby, Christine, who would become the pride and joy of his life. Anji and I, of course, then became foster grandparents at 25 years of age. Even today I still do a double-take when Christine calls me "Poppy".

Denise and baby moved in with us and Metus moved back to his grandparents for a while. He would often come over, but he was beginning to be unwell with a number of psychiatric episodes.

Still when he was clear minded enough I would teach him how to read using the Bible and write using an old typewriter. He would watch the Jesus video countless times and he would question us about our faith. We would talk till late into the night about what being a Christian meant. Metus once tried to talk Giovanni, a local man who lived in the bus shelter at the end of our street, into moving in with us, "because that is what Jesus would do," he said. The man was not amused at the suggestion, but he did become Metus' friend, that is, until his sad and untimely death on the streets, apparently because of alcohol poisoning. But Metus' familiarity with the gospels had some unexpected consequences. After one of his psychiatric episodes, the local hospital staff were driven mad by his constant quoting of verses from the gospels as if he actually were Jesus. So I was not the most popular visitor with the staff when they found out I was the minister who had taught him these scriptures.

Metus' life gradually became more confusing for him and his world grew darker and darker. He was sniffing aerosols constantly, had just started to dabble in heroin and had repeated psychotic episodes. He was hearing voices telling him to hurt those he loved and I can remember trying to convince him that there were no huge faces in the trees outside Denise's flat. Over the years, I took him to more than a hundred meetings with doctors, social workers and psychologists. He lived in hospitals, juvenile detention centres and group homes. He was diagnosed with an intellectual disability, a psychosis and then drug addiction. He did not fit one convenient category, was often uncooperative and was regularly moved on to be someone else's problem.

Many of us tried to help and love Metus and I can think of no-one for whom more prayers were said. However, on Wednesday, 22 April 1998, Metus died of a drug overdose. He died alone in an abandoned house near the local Clayton railway station, covered in paint and surrounded by needles. The darkness of his world had overcome him. He was just 18 years old.

I said my goodbyes to Metus at his funeral. It was a Cook Island traditional funeral and I shared leading the service with a Cook Island minister. The tradition is to have an open casket allowing mourners to express their feelings directly to the deceased as if they were listening. I looked down at his still body and kissed his cold forehead as he lay in the casket. 'We loved you Metus' I cried out, 'We really did. You didn't change. You didn't get better. You got worse.' I realized even then, however, that a change had happened. 'You didn't change… but I did mate. Know that I will dedicate my life to do all I can to see others have life.'

While we hope and dream for change in others as we share compassion, another kind of miracle often happens in our lives. We are the ones impacted and transformed by seeking to love through Jesus. Others don't always change the way we hope they will, but we are transformed as we cope with them not changing. Metus had not changed in the way we'd hoped for but I was a different person and something new was birthed. Urban Neighbours Of Hope (UNOH) actually began a year after we met Metus. We entered his world of urban poverty and found we needed God's vulnerable love in places and people that were not working. In so many ways UNOH is part of Metus' legacy as it continues on 20 years later. There are no guaranteed outcomes as we follow Jesus into compassion, but compassion is never wasted.

If we are to be disciples of Jesus we must remember why Jesus came. The very purpose of the Spirit's anointing is not to build bigger churches, but to transform. It was *transformation* that Jesus talked about when he announced his mission in Nazareth. Returning from forty days of fasting "in the power of the Spirit", Jesus stood up in a local synagogue and read from the scroll of the prophet Isaiah:

> The Spirit of the Lord is upon me, because he has anointed me to bring good news to the poor. He has sent me to proclaim release to the captives and recovery of sight to the blind, to let the oppressed go free, to proclaim the year of the Lord's favour." And he rolled up the scroll, gave it back to the attendant, and sat down. The eyes of all in the synagogue were fixed on him. Then he began to say to them, "Today this scripture has been fulfilled in your hearing.
>
> Luke 4:18-21

The kind of transformation Jesus teaches is an ongoing and dynamic process of people, groups and systems living together as God intends in the midst of a fallen world. Jesus' anointed and transforming mission is about the struggles, breakthroughs and gifts of God's will being done on earth as it is in heaven. As Jesus clearly announced, the litmus test of transformation is whether we're proclaiming Good News to the poor or not. In Jesus' economy, if the poor have authentic good news it will trickle up to the whole world.

Typically, we do not immediately think that the Holy Spirit's first impulse is to proclaim that the oppressed are liberated. In fact, we have to admit, Christians haven't always followed Jesus' heartbeat and mission expressed at Nazareth. For example, Shane Claiborne once surveyed a group of 'strong followers of Jesus' asking, "Did Jesus spend time with the poor?" Eighty percent replied yes. Just think for a moment about the people with whom Jesus did life, miracles, death and resurrection, and it is shocking that twenty percent missed it. I mean, what kind of gospel are they reading? Shane also asked this same group, "Do you spend time with the poor?" This time only two percent replied, yes. If these numbers are a true reflection, and I think they might be, this has to be one of the greatest tragedies of our time. The transforming power of the Spirit on his people is being kept from the world, with the most vulnerable missing out on an opportunity to live. Are too many just talking to, and about Jesus and the Holy Spirit, but not actually following them on mission?

The bigger question this raises for me is why there is such a disconnection between Jesus' mission and the lives of those who claim his Spirit indwells them. I don't believe Christians avoid the poor because they lack compassion or are unaware of Jesus' core concerns. Perhaps a key reason comes from seeing others in misery and not knowing what to do about it. That moment of cluelessness strikes such fear in the human heart that even Christians sometimes try to organize their lives in order to avoid it. Henri Nouwen challenges us concerning the kind of compassion that can overcome these moments:

> Let us not underestimate how hard it is to be compassionate.

> Compassion is hard because it requires the inner disposition to go with others to the place where they are weak, vulnerable, lonely, and broken. But this is not our spontaneous response to suffering. What we desire most is to do away with suffering by fleeing from it or finding a quick cure for it. As busy, active, relevant ministers, we want to earn our bread by making a real contribution. This means first and foremost doing something to show that our presence makes a difference. And so we ignore our greatest gift which is our ability to enter into solidarity with those who suffer. Those who can sit in silence with their fellowman, not knowing what to say but knowing that they should be there, can bring new life in a dying heart. Those who are not afraid to hold a hand in gratitude, to shed tears in grief and to let a sigh of distress arise straight from the heart can break through paralysing boundaries and witness the birth of a new fellowship, the fellowship of the broken.

When we'd rather be competent than fools for Christ we miss sharing our 'greatest gift,' vulnerability, personal solidarity with Jesus among the poor, where the transforming Spirit is released. To minister to the 'fellowship of the broken' we need the help of other Jesus-fools so we can keep finding, learning and growing in Christ-like responses.

Over the years a practice we found that has helped provide space for compassion was 'open homes.' We now live in Winson Green, Birmingham, UK. This multiracial, inner city neighborhood is where some of the first urban industrialized neighborhoods began over two hundred years ago. It was the seedbed for the industrial revolution, where the first steam engines and modern factories where developed, but is now a place needing urgent renewal and re-imagination. Perhaps best known for the 1400 prisoners incarcerated in HMP Birmingham and the controversial Channel 4 documentary series 'Benefits Street,' Winson Green provides an important, live context for honest personal growth and urban engagement.

Winson Green is also where Lesslie Newbigin (1909-1998) served as a Minister in the 1980s after he returned from thirty years of Christian service in India. While in Winson Green, Newbigin wrote such influential books as *Gospel in a Pluralist Society*, *The Open Secret* and *Foolishness to the Greeks*. A man before his time, he articulated the tough urban questions and dedicated his life to finding and living the answers in both Majority and Western World urban contexts. It is hoped that Newbigin's life and insights will inspire a new generation of Christian workers able to respond to growing urban injustices in our day and to help see abundant community cultivated from the ground up around the world. The Newbigin family gave special permission for *Newbigin House* and *Newbigin School for Urban Leadership* to be named in honor of Lesslie Newbigin.

One of the first things we have done here in Birmingham, UK is set up a home for hospitality. We moved our family into the Newbigin House building, a 7 bedroom former Vicarage in the heart of the neighborhood, and within 2 months enjoyed over 300 people coming together for meals, meetings and mayhem, not to mention enjoying the alpacas! Co-operative dreams, plans and actions have more than begun!

To make our home in neighborhoods like Winson Green and to invite people to come and share our lives and homes has been some of the most difficult but rewarding quality times of our life as a family. We have found that Isaiah 61:1-4 inspires our work and life together as neighbors in Winson Green and Handsworth. It speaks of people and places seeing 'restoration,' 'renewal' and 'rebuilding.' This includes people who have experienced 'oppression,' 'broken heartedness,' 'captivity,' 'prison' and 'grief' of which many in our neighborhood are familiar. There is a vision here of swapping 'ashes for beauty,' 'sorrow for joy' and 'hope for despair.'. As neighbors we too want to be like 'oaks of justice,' 'well planted' and 'growing stronger.' We long to see Newbigin House become like a seedbed for urban change, enabling opportunities for neighbors to express gifts, passions and dreams as a basis for renewing our common life together in Winson Green and Handsworth.

I am not sure how many foster children, adults and teenagers have lived with us over the years in Melbourne, Bangkok and now Birmingham or had meals with us. It may well be in the thousands? Jesus helped us see that family needed to be more than nuclear to be healthy. If the Gospel can never be privatized, then neither can lives that seek to follow the Gospel.

For so many urbanites, however, attempts to separate sacred and secular, ministry and private life, makes space for Jesus to fill our home with 'the other' difficult. Yet the risks and the shifts are worth it. Jesus' priorities as seen in open homes were constantly put to us, and not just left to some far off time when we can could around to it.

We have found that open homes can provide a tangible centre for living out the Gospel in cities. Where isolation, alienation and despair tear apart, the connection of hospitality can heal and reconcile. It was Jesus invitation to share hospitality that opens Zacchaeus to be converted to share what he has with others. Further, Jesus said explicitly that at the end of the age he was actually encountered among those who were seeking accommodation, invited to dinner, needing clothes and visits. (Matthew 25:31ff). We need a good excuse to reject Jesus in these disguises. Sometimes we did need space as a family and while our homes in Bangkok were smaller than in Melbourne we still loved having people share our lives with us.

In some ways Newbigin House is better equipped for community living as we find new ways to share hospitality. We may not always entertain angels unaware, but there are miracles in these connections. Many of those we include in our lives experience transformation. Some even became beacons of hope, not just for themselves but for others too. We never forget however, that it's also miraculous when God transforms us to keep learning to love and cope with others who are not changing. If true compassion is "suffering with" then such practices as hospitality and open homes can shine a light on the areas we need to grow to mature and be more Christ-like.

Christian conversion always makes conversion to the poor a required subject. Those on the edge and the bottom are not an elective in the Reign the God. This conversion though, is not just about our conversion to make us feel less guilty. True guilt is the nerve endings of the soul, so we need to listen to our conscience less we become lepers in the ethical sense. No, this conversion is about changing the lives of the poor through the authority of Jesus. Guilt might wake you up, but making a difference in the lives of the poor will keep you on the adventure with Jesus.

We find that Jesus is the only hope for the poor. A biblical understanding of poverty is not just about lack of cash or lack of spirituality. Poverty is about oppression. Oppression externally and internally that only the authority of Jesus can deliver people, groups and systems from.

Have we experienced this conversion to the poor lately? Have we encountered Jesus in the eyes of actual people facing poverty and joined their fight for liberation from oppression?

3. Converted to Community

"a descendent of Abraham too" (v9)

The third conversion of discipleship in our new urban world is being converted to *community*. Jesus announces that Zacchaeus is, "A descendent of Abraham too" (v9). Community is about a sense of belonging that is crucial in seeing transformation occur. It is interesting that in Mark's Gospel there is no singular term 'disciple'. It is always '*disciples*', for we need community in the midst of transformation and transitions.

What Zacchaeus quickly found in redistributing his wealth and sharing hospitality with those who are marginalized was that he couldn't do it alone. The fact that Jesus affirms Zacchaeus is part of the family of Abraham is crucial. If a conversion to Jesus to encounter and follow is crucial for Christians, then personally joining his agenda with those facing urban injustices is crucial. How we do that in a sustainable way is also important. The nature of Christian faith is communal, not only that our God is Trinity, but a collective witness is required for change. In our urbanising world community building is not intuitive and this needs further exploration.

Post-modern, globalized urban culture inherently nurtures a need for individuals to feel special, separate and superior. Indeed, two hundred years of conditioning for radicalized individualism and three decades of systematic marketing means each person now feels entitled to the best in life because, 'we are worth it'. We are now far more ready to defend our own image created for cyberspace, than be ready with the sensitivity and maturity needed to love others in our own neighborhood. These cultural conditions create challenges to building any real sense of community with others, be they in church, or indeed any other voluntary or unpaid association.

This conditioning, though initiated and incubated in the West, is spreading. A rising number of Majority World people, now birthed in and conditioned by a rapidly urbanizing, consumer global culture, are also finding personal image easier to maintain than sharing life with those crowded around them. Over 1 billion people, around 1 in 6 people, live in urban slums like Klong Toey and yet we are all overwhelmed by the same marketing as in the West. It may be more overwhelming because there are simply no limits. I could walk out of my front door in Klong Toey and look up beyond the corrugated iron rooftops, tangles of illegal electrical wires and jutting TV antennas and see a flood lit, tennis-court sized billboard, advertising the latest condominium you really must have if you want the good life. Nurtured with the same desires and expectations as the rich but without the where-with-all to even touch that lifestyle, this radical inequality is creating a poisonous resentment in the burgeoning urban poor. Added to this there is also a bubbling guilt that my neighbors felt A sense that they weren't quite good enough to join that life just beyond their reach. That maybe, if they just cared more, worked harder, drank less or were smarter they could join the high society. However, the reasoning goes, someone else must be to blame for my lack for surely, I am so special! In this context is it any wonder we see so many violent street riots. Surely, we have not even begun to see the start of the urban unrest, instability and environmental disasters that will ensue, as these unsustainable lifestyles are pursued by individuals at all costs.

What then can Christian faith and mission offer to these serious global and local challenges that threaten to de-humanize us?

As Zacchaeus' conversion shows us Christian discipleship is not primarily about general statements of belief or intent, but a particular kind of sharing life. The core thread of the biblical narrative is to love our particular God with particular neighbors in a particular place. Yet, sharing life with others is simply foreign to most of us.

Indeed, even the basic practices for community living are almost a lost art, even for Christians. Christine Pohl, for example, researched what helped and hindered Christian community building, and identified four crucial practices. (Pohl, 2011). It is hard not to compare these four practices with contemporary values. Where 'nurturing a sense of gratitude' helps build a sense of community, a sense of entitlement often pervades. Where 'making and keeping promises' helps build the trust needed to share life together, we see the norm as keeping all options open in case something better comes along. Where 'truth telling' helps us grow and mature, we see spin control and image management by even our best leaders. Where 'sharing hospitality' opens us to others not like us (and therefore who we really are), we see a tribalism that seeks only its own advantage, blaming any woes on outsiders (and therefore in denial about who our tribe really is).

This lack of experience and aptitude in community building affects the

Body of Christ as much as the wider world. Indeed, a lack of maturity in sharing life with others has undermined many good urban missional projects. You can see it when even the most gifted people refuse to pick up responsibilities, take initiative or push through difficult tasks and seasons in life. It's easier to take my bat and ball and play somewhere else than go deeper with God, people and place.

This conditioning is especially a problem for those who want to end poverty and injustice. As Jayakuma Christian explains poverty is the result of relationships that don't work, principally the god complexes of the non-poor oppressing the poor (Christian, 2011). Even our best ideas and intentions then, can undermine transformation because god complexes, thinking we are all powerful, centers of the universe, reinforce more oppressive relationships. You see this especially in development industry marketing: if you just give £30 a month you will end poverty for this child. We know vulnerability, suffering and oppression are far more sinister than a spare change problem. This is not to say we shouldn't work or advocate for justice, but the power dynamic relationship between poor and non-poor is a complex one that requires humility, maturity and change on both sides.

A practice we have found key is to take seriously community formation. Over the years, we have found some common practices, disciplines and rhythms of life that can offer a container to help us grow in maturity, for life, community and sustainable mission in and through Jesus. We call this process community formation and it helps individuals and communities to name their expectations of each other at different stages in their development. This container helps people 'stay put', facing themselves in Jesus, rather than avoiding or distracting themselves into superficiality.

Jesus of Nazareth did not simply proclaim a message. He built a community in the power of the Spirit that could multiply his discipleship movement and sustain his transformative vision that God's Kingdom is at hand (Mt. 12:28, Mk. 1:15, Lk. 10:9, Jn. 14:12, Acts 1:8). Jesus called people to leave family and friends to join a new set of family and friends and demonstrated that it takes an empowered, committed community to reach a community (Mt. 10:35-40, Mk. 10:29-30, Lk. 9:23, Jn. 12:24-25, Acts 2 and 4). This kind of committed team dynamic is also crucial if Christians are to experience a sense of the incarnational dynamic of God and see long-term transformation happen in urban neighborhoods. Community is a sense of belonging that is the fruit of common commitments and personal investment. It's crucial then those common commitments are named and their meanings explored with those who experience this belonging. These are time-consuming starting points for new workers and their communities, but essential if our consumer conditioning is to be reset and resisted.

Inspired by ancient Celtic orders and successive waves of committed, covenanted Christian communities through the centuries, we have found life together makes a difference; that our collective witness is far more effective in the long-term than individual heroism. We have found that committing to some specific lifestyle practices together can free members from guessing whether they are "in" or "out" since the pathway is clear and up front, with clear markers and boundaries on the way. For example, the first level for our UNOH community was a one year apprenticeship. The aims of the apprenticeship were to enable the apprentice to have a lived experience of our community and for us to clarify if the gifts of that individual are compatible with the gifts of our order. The bonding with both the existing order members and neighbors were the priority of this first year more than any ministry results. While there were some action reflection and study groups, ministry responsibilities, and participation in common practices, the apprenticeship is not considered a long-term investment by the Order or the apprentice.

In May 2012 I got to meet Jean Vanier, the founder and spiritual leader of L'Arche communities who now have communities of people with disabilities in over a hundred countries. His tall, 80 year old frame, just glowed Jesus. He was kind enough to have read my PhD on the rise of slums and did the Foreword to the published version of *Slum Life Rising*

(Barker, 2012). and I was there to thank him. He was genuinely interested in the rise of slums, and at one point said, 'This is so terrible. What is happening to millions, the Mafia control, the fate of children. It's terrible. You do know though don't you, you are not a solution to this, but you can be a sign.' I found that liberating, helping to challenge my own god complexes and maturity. Our community building is not the final solution for urban poverty, but we can be a sign of hope for what God wants done in the world.

Perhaps it is not going too far to suggest that the Church will rise and fall on its ability to do community formation with the emerging generations. Without it there will be a self-destruction through immaturity. Skills are not enough in these times and character-lessons take time to develop in people. If new communities are going to be the new wine-skins required for our urban world, then it would seem impossible without taking seriously intentional, spiritual, community formation.

4. Converted to place:

'A descendant of Abraham too'

Abraham's call by God was not just to community but be a particular people in a particular promised land. To be loyal to that land and that place is both a promise and a hope. That sense of sustainable belonging for Zacchaeus was about a community of people, but also about belonging to a place.

In many contemporary Christian expressions, the role of place or land has no significance. There is a sense that people and Jesus matter, but not the places they share. One of the important emphasis of Christian discipleship is the taking of urban places seriously. Why? Because urban neighborhoods are created places. As such, God is present and each local place has a sacredness about it that requires nurture and attention, especially by local Christians. A conversion and call to radical locality, therefore, should be an integral part of any urban mission approach if real transformation is to occur.

This call to place is crucial for all parts of the city. Sociologist Robert Putnam has explored the loss of community and the decline in civil engagement and social capital in America. He identifies four key factors contributing to the decline: pressures on time and money; suburbanization, commuting and sprawl; electronic entertainment; and generational changes (Putnam, 2000). These factors disproportionately affect poor, urban neighborhoods, but are a warning to all:

> While... the erosion of social capital and community engagement has affected Grosse Point in essentially the same degree as inner-city Detroit, the impact of that development has so far been greater in the inner city, which lacks the cushioning of other forms of capital. The shooting sprees that affected schools in suburban and rural communities as the twentieth century ended are a reminder that as breakdown of community continues in more privileged settings, affluence and education are insufficient to prevent collective tragedy (Putnam, 2000, p.318).

These forces of globalized culture affect all people and the local Christian church is no exception. To survive, most churches have needed to become more regional than local. In a fascinating article, Matt Cleaver mused that while the idea of vocation in churches has moved beyond the Christian professional and includes living out faith in all of life, the strength of the newly-accepted model is often lost because of the lack of local connection:

> I wonder how many have taught, and more importantly lived, vocation as living out your faith literally *where you are located.* One of the problems with speaking of vocation in such a way is that our churches are anything but local. I drive about 25 minutes to the church where I work. There are nine ELCA churches closer to my house

> than the one to which we belong, one of them only a mile and a half away. I know the vast majority of parishioners drive past dozens of churches before arriving at worship on Sunday. To become a local church again, there would have to be major changes to existing churches or church plants that intentionally work out of a value of locality and close proximity (Cleaver, 2008).

As a response to these very real contemporary human challenges, recent times have seen the development of a theology of local places. Walter Brueggemann is one contributor to the discussion, drawing a distinction between pursuing space and a sense of place:

> 'Space' means an arena of freedom, without coercion or accountability, free of pressures and void of authority. Space may be imagined as a weekend, holiday, and is characterized by a kind of neutrality or emptiness waiting to be filled by our choosing. Such a concern appeals to a desire to get out from under meaningless routine and subjection. But 'place' is a very different matter. Place is space that has historical meanings, where some things have happened that are now remembered and that provide continuity and identity across generations. Place is space in which important words have been spoken that have established identity, defined vocation, and envisioned destiny. Place is space in which vows have been exchanged, promises have been made, and demands have been issued. Place is indeed a protest against the unpromising pursuit of space. It is a declaration that our humanness cannot be found in escape, detachment, absence of commitment, and undefined freedom (Brueggemann, 1977, (2004 edition), p.4).

A perspective which views slum and squatter neighborhood transformation in terms of a move from 'space' to 'place' has much to offer. It builds on the relating, the humility, the learning and the supporting of previous initiatives, as discussed above, but goes further. Seeing neighborhoods in their entirety as sacred places, worth both preserving and improving can change the way Christians view slums. Slums, as the location of relationships, need to find a humanness and divinity if transformation is to occur. A number of benefits can accrue from a focus on neighborhoods as sacred places for Christians to share.

First, the most ancient forms of Christian faith knew well the importance of place for discipleship and mission. This is a theme taken up by Jonathan Wilson-Hartgrove in his book *The Wisdom of Stability*: 'Our spiritual growth depends on human beings rooting ourselves in a place on earth with other creatures' (Wilson-Hartgrove, 2010, p.4). He notes that the early church was 'together in one place' as they shared to such a degree that 'no one was in need' (Acts 2 and 4). This may well have been an unusual moment in Christian history. Thoughts of Christ's imminent return could have been a factor influencing their generosity. The point, however, is not lost. When Christians connect with the incarnating God in real local places together, radical sharing and transformation is possible. Wilson-Hartgrove also cites Anthony, an early church father, who simply said: 'In whatever place you find yourself, do not easily leave it' (Wilson-Hartgrove, 2010, p.35). Another advised similarly, 'If a trial comes upon you in the place where you live, do not leave that place when the trial comes. Wherever you go, you will find that what you are running from is ahead of you' (Wilson-Hartgrove, 2010, p.35). We cannot run away from God or from our own selves. Christians can only find themselves in Christ with others when they stop and stay long enough to share their lives.

Second, a focus on local slum neighborhoods as shared place can also have benefits in terms of church growth. This view has been taken up in some recent literature. For example, in reflecting on the early disciples' sense of community, 'that they were in one place' (Acts 2:1), Randy Frazee writes,

> The re-discovery of neighborhood is the essential application to discovering a common place. It is really the only option. Why? Because it it's the only way we can attain the characteristics that produce authentic community, such as spontaneity, availability and frequency (Frazee, 2001, p.158).

The early church did not just meet as an occasional regional network of individuals. Rather, it was a daily, all of life, experience, not possible without the spontaneity, availability and frequency that living near each other provided. Neighborhood locations may not be the 'only option' as Frazee contends, but they may well be the best possible focus for slum transformations and churches based within them.

Third, Christian presence rooted in a place has very practical, sociological benefits and possibilities too. Robert Putman notes, for example, that positive, stable families who live in poor neighborhoods can influence whole neighborhoods. He writes:

> Just as neighborhoods can affect families, so can families affect neighborhoods. In economists' terms, family social capital has 'positive externalities', spilling out of the home and into the streets. In Northern California scholars have found that the presence of lots of stable families in a neighborhood is associated with lower levels of youthful lawbreaking, not because the adults serve as role models or supervisors, but because the adults rear well-adjusted and well behaved kids. Thus, 'good families' have a ripple effect by increasing the pool of 'good peers' that other families' kids can befriend. If we think of youthful troublemaking as a communicable disease - a sort of behavioural chicken pox that spreads through high schools and friendship groups - then stable families provide the vaccines that reduce the number of contagious kids capable of infecting others (Putnam, 2000, p.314).

When Christians consider what they have to offer in response to slum and squatter neighborhoods, relocation to be present in a particular local place over time should be considered as an option with great potential for bringing about transformation. This is the case not least in slums, which often have little cushioning for the lack of social capital they typically experience. A real living presence in a place with little social capital can help to bring about transformation.

Fourth, to focus on slum neighborhoods as place rather than space can also have potential positive economic and environmental impacts. This is a theme taken up by Wendal Berry's call for self-sufficient neighborhoods (Berry, 2002). If communities can grow their own food and work toward economic independence they can then be free to be interdependent with other neighborhoods, thus reducing the economic and environmental costs of transporting food and other goods. Berry's work often has rural places in mind, but community gardens based on roofs and local cooperatives are just as possible in slums as in rural lands. A fundamental shift from consumer to citizen does need to take place, however, as McKnight and Block make clear (McKnight and Block, 2010). Christians can have a particular hope that such shifts toward neighborhood self-sufficiency are possible if it is understood that the Creator is present, the Spirit can empower, and Jesus can be followed.

How can the incarnational call to place work out in practice? When as UNOH workers we took stock of our first ten years as a movement, we saw that our ideals, values and passions best lent themselves to local neighborhoods. We would drive around desperately trying to generate a community to empower and disciple, but this quickly wore us out. Taking neighborhoods seriously helped us to focus our vocation and life together in ways that were sustainable and helped us to go deeper with people.

An image that UNOH first adopted around 2003 to help us focus was that of urban villages centred on Christ as the communal dimension of our mission. The metaphor, however inspiring, also threatened us as UNOH workers. The sense of belonging, connection and peace the image of village conveys is also matched by the fear of personally being found wanting. If the most appealing aspect of village life is the possibility of being known as we really are, then the least appealing aspect of village life is also the possibility of being known as we really are. Yet, there is no way around this challenge. If we are to share Christ incarnationally in place then our own weakness and vulnerability is required.

Our focus on how neighborhoods could become villages centered on Christ required some definitional work. First, we defined a neighborhood as a common area that neighbors can walk around. Since the poor often do not have their own vehicles or need to use them sparsely, it was crucial that we define neighborhood by the following test: could a neighbor walk to each neighbor's house easily? By this definition the Kelvin Grove neighborhood in Springvale was really one whole neighborhood block. In Bangkok our first neighborhood focus was really Jet Sip Rye, rather than the whole of Klong Toey.

Second, there were a number of indicators we began to notice when our localities began to become like villages centered on Christ. These included our neighbors being available to:

Celebrate together: times of birthday parties, weddings and so on;

Commiserate together: times of loss, death and grief;

Have common meals, including Communion, together: times of fellowship around a meal;

Resolve conflict together: times of clarity and learning to live together;

Be there in times of change together: times of getting to know new neighbors and passage of life changes;

Be there in times of crisis together: times of being out of control and banding together;

Share common goods together: time of sharing what we

have with others who don't have;

Share common prayers together: time to pray for people as a normal part of life;

Share a common identity from living in a common place together: time to see each neighbor as part of the same village;

Affirm community contributions: times to let leaders lead in their own areas of responsibility and giftedness and celebrate these contributions (Barker, 2003, p.4-5).

All of these events can happen at any time in a neighborhood. Most can't be scheduled in a busy timetable. Dave Andrews explains the difference between *chronos* time and *kairos* time in community building in a way that relates specially to slum life:

> The Bible warns us not to be so preoccupied with what it calls the chronos, or 'the time' that we miss what it calls the kairos, 'the moments', when people are more open than closed and we have the opportunities to develop significant relationships with one another. These kairos moments often pass as quickly as they come. So, it's important that we grasp these moments when they come our way - otherwise we risk losing the opportunities they present forever (Andrews, 2006, p.116).

To seek to be attentive and present in our neighborhoods for such sacred space-sharing moments and to support them prayerfully and physically has become crucial in transformation. A part of our covenant together, became that even on our busiest days we would spend at least one third of the day in our neighborhoods. These kinds of commitments to neighborhood presence have ensured realistic focus and have made a difference

We need a vision for our cities as places of redemption. The motifs of eternal life, salvation and Kingdom of God are such important threads in the Gospel's rich tapestry that we unstitch them at our own peril. Indeed, one of the most important contemporary Lukan scholars argues that:

> Throughout, the Lukan narrative focuses attention on a pervasive, coordinating theme: salvation. Salvation is neither ethereal nor merely future, but embraces life in the present, restoring the integrity of human life, revitalizing human communities, setting the cosmos in order, and commissioning the community of God's people to put God's grace into practice among themselves and toward ever-widening circles of others. The Third Evangelist knows nothing of such dichotomies as those sometimes drawn between social and spiritual or individual and communal. Salvation embraces the totality of embodied life, including its social, economic, and political concerns (Green, 1997).

The Romans were the latest in a long line of oppressor-rulers and God's people were anxious for real life to start and have no end. This new life was promised in the Hebrew history, law and prophets. For example, we see Isaiah 65:17-25, promise very new physical and social realities that the Hebrew people expected to inherit.

> *'For I am about to create new heavens*
> *and a new earth;*
> *the former things shall not be remembered*
> *or come to mind.*
> *But be glad and rejoice for ever*
> *in what I am creating;*
> *for I am about to create Jerusalem as a joy,*
> *and its people as a delight.*
> *I will rejoice in Jerusalem,*
> *and delight in my people;*
> *no more shall the sound of weeping be heard in it,*
> *or the cry of distress.*
> *No more shall there be in it*
> *an infant that lives but a few days,*

or an old person who does not live out a lifetime;
for one who dies at a hundred years will be considered a
youth,
and one who falls short of a hundred will be considered
accursed.
They shall build houses and inhabit them;
they shall plant vineyards and eat their fruit.
They shall not build and another inhabit;
they shall not plant and another eat;
for like the days of a tree shall the days of my people be,
and my chosen shall long enjoy the work of their hands.
They shall not labour in vain,
or bear children for calamity;
for they shall be offspring blessed by the LORD*—*
and their descendants as well.
Before they call I will answer,
while they are yet speaking I will hear.
The wolf and the lamb shall feed together,
the lion shall eat straw like the ox;
but the serpent—its food shall be dust!
They shall not hurt or destroy
on all my holy mountain,
says the LORD*.*

God promises here sustainable and resilient life in a particular place including employment, health and how the most vulnerable people and the land itself are empowered and healed. This is what God intends when the spheres of heaven and earth come together to form a new creation. Indeed, it is a promise of what God will do through the Hebrew people. When will this great day would come? It is not a question about other-worldly, disembodied evacuation plans to heaven as many of us imagine when we hear the words 'eternal life'. The Biblical witness uses different metaphors for this 'eternal life'. These include 'shalom', 'salvation' and 'Kingdom of God'. These are all ways of saying that God's intended peace and love is fulfilled in relationship between God, people and the earth. It is a vision for the here and now that is never lost.

Biblical visions for our future are important foundations for our work in cities. If we build or work on illusions and superstitions our lives are easily wasted. As I try to evaluate my years of urban ministry there is a scripture that quickly comes to mind. It's about how our work will be tested by fire and only what is good and true will last. (1 Cor. 3:12-14) So much of my service was not built with gold, but 'wood, hay and straw' and will be lost. I do believe that all truth is God's and only what has joined with Jesus remains, the rest will be forgotten. Where have I joined in with the eternal now and where have I only been distracted or compulsive? These are tough, but important, ultimate questions to consider.

If I were to name my biggest change theologically in my Klong Toey years it would be my approach to the material and especially to place. I had inherited a dichotomy that the spiritual life was crucial and the material didn't really matter that much. As I began to pray, read and reflect informed by our context I came to believe all material is sacred and is being redeemed by God. God called the physical creation into being and exclaimed that it is 'very good'. This creation project, however, will only be completed when all evil is defeated and creation is fully alive with the glory and knowledge of God 'as the waters cover the sea' (Isaiah 11:9). Just as the sea is already water, God's presence will one day be 'all in all' (1 Corinthians 15:28). Hope for the renewal of creation and the physical, then, is fundamental to the Christian ideas of both compassion and hope. Where we believe the story is going matters for how we invest our lives now.

I need to credit N. T. Wright with opening my eyes to this understanding and vision for the material future. His book *Surprised by Hope* rattled, inspired and made me realize I didn't know what I was really aiming for in Klong Toey. When we saw so much premature death around us what did I believe about life and death for those neighbors dying around me? Eternal life, Wright argues, is to fully live in the life after life after death.

We do suffer and die, but what we do in this life through Jesus will live on when we are bodily resurrected and all creation is perfected in love. One day all creation will be resurrected because God's shalom has begun in Jesus' resurrection and no act of compassion will be wasted.

Corinthians 15:58 once more:

> what you do in the Lord is not in vain. You are not oiling the wheels of a machine that's about to roll over a cliff. You are not restoring a great painting that's shortly going to be thrown on the fire. You are not planting roses in a garden that's about to be dug up for a building site. You are- strange though it may seem, almost as hard to believe as the resurrection itself – accomplishing something that will become in due course part of God's new world. Every act of love, gratitude, and kindness; every work of art of music inspired by the love of God and delight in the beauty of his creation; every minute spent teaching a severely handicapped child to read or to walk; every act of care and nurture, of comfort and support for one's fellow human beings and for that matter one's fellow nonhuman creatures; and of course every prayer, all Spirit-led teaching, every deed that spreads the gospel, builds up the church, embraces and embodies holiness rather than corruption, and makes the name of Jesus honored in the world – all of this will find its way, through the resurrecting power of God, into a new creation that God will one day make. That is the logic of and the mission of God. God's recreation of his wonderful world, which began with the resurrection of Jesus and continues mysteriously as God's people live in the risen Christ and by the Spirit in the present is not wasted. It will last all the way into God's new world. In fact, it will be enhanced there (Wright, 2008, p.9).

God by nature infused people and the rest of creation with his presence, but one day the space made for love will be fully returned. Time and space which is now inhabited by rebellion will one day be redeemed and fully filled with the Lord's knowledge and glory. God is present in creation (including in people) before this hope is fulfilled, but the incomplete presence and intensity of God's glory is crucial to recognize in places like slums. It is the presence of God who seeks to fulfil the full hope for and through creation, but has not done so yet.

The kinds of prayers I have mostly prayed in Klong Toey isn't 'how do I save this soul before he dies', but 'Lord, let your Kingdom Come, Your will done, on earth as in heaven. May this hope become reality and start with us right here and now!' It is a comfort to know that even if projects or buildings or even our names are forgotten, what we have done through Jesus will never be obsolete.

Andy Flannagan, an Irish singer-song writer and political activist, once challenged me to envision what Klong Toey would be like when the realms of heaven and earth fully join together one day. This question of vision has energized me in the day to day struggles and helped me see what we were doing was worthwhile even if it was only part of the picture. It's not about schemes to trick people into praying prayers and joining our church, but rather imagining what eternal life could be offered in Klong Toey and what I sought to see happen that could last forever. This is actually what I wrote from Andy's question that put all other questions in its place:

> *Now Klong Toey's people and places so often face deadly diseases, violent disturbances and premature deaths. When That Great Day comes all tears will be wiped away and nothing will be able to stop Klong Toey's people connecting joyfully with the Creator, each other and our land. There will be healthy, fit and happy people who all love playing football together (without referees!) on lush green grass where there used to be open sewers, polluted swamps and dumping areas.*
>
> *Now Klong Toey's people and places are so often easy pickings for*

organized crime, corruption and political cronyism. When That Great Day comes all injustices by people and powers will be put to right in Klong Toey. There will be a fresh start and all relationships will work well for each person's health and wellbeing especially for those who were formerly isolated, exploited or alone.

Now Klong Toey's people and places are often so isolated, exploited and ghettoized from the earth's resources by economic powers. When That Great Day comes Klong Toey will be a Holy city valued and honored an indispensable part of the New Heavens and New Earth. There will be constant awareness of God's universal life giving presence, creative unity and enough for all. A walk down to our market will remind each person deep in their bones that they were made in God's image for a real purpose to offer others.

Lord, let your Kingdom come, let your will be done in Klong Toey as in heaven.

Conclusions: What was Zacchaeus like at the end of the story? Where are we?

Responding to our cities as disciples of Jesus requires conversions. We can't do this on our own, by sheer will power or even smart design. What was Zacchaeus like at the end of the story? Before, he was powerful but after his conversion he had an eternal authority, while still physically vulnerable. Before, he was rich, after, he chose poverty. Before, he was alone, after, he was accepted into a revolutionary community. Before, he was a spectator, after, a player forever remembered in the divine drama.

The Good News is that we can experience these conversions too. Have we been awakened and converted to this Good News of the Kingdom enough to share it with our lives and our words in places like Zacchaeus was? How can we find the containers to incubate such life?

The urgency for Christians to be converted in these ways cannot be over stated. It is no exaggeration to say that Christians could well be found wanting in this new urban world. For example, in an interconnected world, rapidly growing urban slums are a challenge to everyone's global security, equality and stability, but Christians have a special mandate from God to seek God's will done on earth as in heaven (Matthew 6:1). Evangelical faith and mission then is especially challenged in how to respond to this new, urbanizing earth. It is estimated, for example, that only 1 in 500 international missionaries and less than 10,000 national Christian workers focus on slums. Many of our Christian aid and development agencies are now very effective in rural areas, but most struggle in urban slums with even our largest like World Vision spending only1.3% of their 2004 global budget on slum projects. We also know personal relationships are a key part of sharing faith, yet as Todd Johnson of the Centre for Global Christianity reports, among Muslims, Hindus, and Buddhist, the three largest religions other than Christianity and where the growing cities of the 10/40 window dominate less than 14% (or 1 in 7) had personal contact with a Christian. It is not an exaggeration to say evangelical engagement is mostly missing the action in some of the most important, growing cities demographically today.

Will a new generation of Christian disciples rise up to submerge themselves deeply, relationally and strategically to be part of seeing more Zacchaeus like conversions happen?

Many urban Christian activists on the front line today resonate with Jeremiah 29:7, "But seek the shalom of the city where I have sent you into exile, and pray to the Lord on its behalf, for in its shalom you will find your shalom." (NRSV with 'shalom' substituted for 'peace'). The promise of shalom, the wellbeing found in the harmony between God, people and place, is remarkable because the city in this verse that God's people have been asked to live, pray and seek shalom in is none other than Babylon, a city that has the most villainous qualities in the biblical narrative.

Perhaps God is calling more of his people to seek the shalom of the world's cities again, to experience the conversions Zacchaeus did, even move into some of the most challenging urban places? If for no other reason, we get to see God at work in neighbors and neighborhoods and have the chance to find our own shalom, it will be worth it.

Notes

1. E. Stanley Jones, *The Christ of the Indian Road* can be downloaded as pdf in full here: https://open.bu.edu/handle/2144/926
2. Ched Myers, *Discipleship in Mark's Gospel* video can be seen here: https://youtu.be/1__YYIpOZJU
3. Dietrich Bonheoffer, 'The Call to Discipleship' (Chapter 2 of *The Cost of Discipleship*) can be viewed in part on Google Books. https://books.google.co.uk/books?id=NamwoIOJnJkC&pg=PA57&dq=discipleship&source=gbs_toc_r&cad=4#v=onepage&q=discipleship&f=false
4. Eberhard Arnold's *Salt and Light* can be downloaded here: http://www.plough.com/en/ebooks/s/salt-and-light
5. Jurgen Moltmann, "The Church in the Power of the Spirit" lecture audio can be downloaded here: http://moltmanniac.com/jurgen-moltmann-2001-grider-winget-lecture-series-at-nts-audio/
6. NT Wright and 'Life after, life after death' interview can be viewed here: https://www.youtube.com/watch?v=rZC6tbgpsl4

References

Andrews, D. (2006). *Compassionate Community Work: An introductory course for Christians.* Carlisle, England: Piquant.

Barker, A. (2012). *Slum Life Rising: How to enflesh hope within a new urban world.* Melbourne, Australia: Urban Neighbours of Hope.

Barker, A. (2003). *Finding Life in Neighborhood Transformations.* Unpublished manuscript.

Berry, W. (2002). *The Art of Commonplace: The agrarian essays of Wendell Berry.* Berkeley, CA: Counterpoint.

Brueggemann, W. (1977 / 2004). *The Land: Place as gift, promise and challenge in biblical faith.* Minneapolis, MN: Fortress.

Christian, J. (2011). *God of the Empty-Handed: Poverty, power and the Kingdom of God.* Melbourne, Australia: Acorn.

Cleaver, M. (2008). A Theology of Geography: Locality and Proximity. (Weblog post). Retrieved from http://mattcleaver.com/2008/10/22/a-theology-of-geography-locality-and-proximity

Frazee, R. (2001). *The Connecting Church: Beyond small groups to authentic community.* Grand Rapids, MI: Zondervan.

Green, J. (1997). *The Gospel of Luke.* Grand Rapids, MI: Eerdmans.

McKnight, J. & Block, P. (2010). *The Abundant Community: Awakening the power of families and neighborhoods.* San Francisco, CA: Berrett-Koehler.

Pohl, C. (2011). *Living into Community: Cultivating practices that sustain us.* Grand Rapids, MI: Eerdmans.

Putnam, R. (2000). *Bowling Alone: The Collapse and Revival of American Community.* New York, NY: Simon and Schuster.

Wilson- Hartgrove, J. (2010). *The Wisdom of Stability: Rooting faith in a mobile culture.* Brewster, MA: Paraclete Press.

Wright, N.T. (2008). *Surprised by Hope.* London, England: Harper Collins.

Urban Disparity: A Prophetic Response

3

Evelyn Feliciano

This chapter first appeared as chapters 3 and 5 of Evelyn Miranda-Feliciano's book, *Unequal Worlds* (2000). It is used here with permission from the Institute for Studies in Asian Church and Culture.

Treading on Dangerous Places: A Prophetic Model

To be the conscience of society is also to be ambassadors of hope.

Text

MICAH 3:1-12

[1] *Then I said,*
"Listen, you heads of Jacob,
you rulers of the house of Israel.
Should you not know justice?
[2] *you who hate good and love evil;*
who tear the skin from my people

and the flesh from their bones;
³who eat my people's flesh,
strip off their skin
and break their bones in pieces;
who chop them up like meat for the pan,
like flesh for the pot?"

⁴Then they will cry out to the Lord,
but he will not answer them,
At that time he will hide his face from them
because of the evil they have done.

⁵This is what the Lord says:
"As for the prophets
who lead my people astray,
if one feeds them,
they proclaim 'peace';
if he does not,
they prepare to wage war against him.
⁶Therefore night will come over you, without visions,
and darkness, without divination.
The sun will set for the prophets,
and the day will go dark for them.
⁷The seers will be ashamed
and the diviners disgraced.
They will all cover their faces
because there is no answer from God. '
⁸But as for me, I am filled with power,
with the Spirit of the Lord,
and with justice and might,
to declare to Jacob his transgression,
to Israel his sin.

⁹Hear this, you rulers of the house of Jacob,
you rulers of the house of Israel,

who despise justice
and distort all that is right;
[10]who build Zion with bloodshed,
and Jerusalem with wickedness. [11]Her leaders judge
for a bribe,
her priests teach for a price,
and her prophets tell fortunes for money.
Yet they lean upon the Lord and say,
"Is not the Lord among us?
No disaster will come upon us.
[12]Therefore because of you,
Zion will be plowed like a field,
Jerusalem will become a heap of rubble,
the temple hill a mound overgrown with thickets.

MICAH 4:1-4

[1]In the last days
the mountain of the Lord's temple will be established
as chief among the mountains;
it will be raised above the hills,
and peoples will stream to it.
[2]Many nations will come and say,
"Come, let us go up to the mountain of the Lord,
to the house of the God of Jacob.
He will teach us his ways,
so that we may walk in his paths."
The law will go out from Zion,
the word of the Lord from Jerusalem.
[3]He will judge between many peoples
and will settle disputes for strong nations far and wide.
They will beat their swords into plowshares
and their spears into pruning hooks.
Nations will not take up sword against nation,
nor will they train for war anymore.

[4]Every man will sit under his own vine
and under his own fig tree,
and no one will make them afraid,
for the Lord Almighty has spoken."

Questions on the text

1. Biblical scholars label Micah as one of the "minor" prophets, yet based on the text, he has a major message. What is his message about, and to what three groups in society is he addressing his message? (3:1-2, 5, 9)

2. What is he particularly condemning in each group? (3:2-3; 5, 9-11) What specific punishments is he predicting for each of them? (3:4, 6-7, 12)

3. What moral authority does Micah claim for himselfsuch that he has the courage to call to task these three groups of national leaders in society? (3:8)

4. Micah's message of condemnation is balanced by his message of hope. (4: 1-4) What is this message? How is it to be realized?

5. Basing on his pronouncements against the leaders of his day, what kind of a man was Micah? How could we be like him today? What is a true prophet?

Comments on the Text (Part 1)

Background on the Prophets

The so-called prophets these days come in many varieties. There is a kind who speaks stridently with nothing but gloom and doom, walking around in a flowing robe. He tends to grab you by the collar, shouting into your ears, "Prepare to meet your God!"

Another comes with a mellifluous voice, and a telegenic personality claiming to have a large telechurch. He/she pleads for telesupport, and people who believe they go to church via their remote control do give considerably. Then one day one hears about the scam this "prophet" is enmeshed in or the immorality tainting his life.

The more common variety is one who walks around with eyes toward heaven, straining his ears to hear the voice of God, and seeing esoteric visions. He asks his followers to abandon family, work and the world to barricade themselves in some "holy ground" because destruction is to come to the whole earth at a specific time on a specific day. And when nothing comes out ofthe prediction, the so-called "prophet" conveniently sets another date.

Was Micah any different from these self-proclaimed prophets?

The prophetic ministry in biblical times was a respectable institution, although like today, false prophets there were, too. It owed its ethical and social concems from Moses. As one of the greatest prophetic lawgivers, Moses outlined the most humane and philanthropic code of the ancient world in the book of Deuteronomy. Micah belongs to that honorable tradition of men and women who played the role of being society's "social conscience." They brought the Word of the Lord to bear upon society's disobedience against God, its injustices against others, and its other moral and social sins that caused rottenness to the national soul. They would sound off a call to repentance and reformation. But they would also draw up the dire consequences of disobedience and transgression.

Therefore, the study of Micah—his life, deeds and words may give us pointers on the possible responses that we could make in the face of the many acts of injustice in our society today. For it is amazing to discover that despite the distance of history and differences in context between Micah's world and ours, we share similar social struggles between the rich and the poor, and between the powerful and the weak.

Micah's world

Micah belonged to the league of "minor" prophets which simply means that his body of works is small unlike the prophet Isaiah's or Jeremiah's. But in his short extant writings, Micah has given Christianity two of the loveliest visions of the future: the birth of the Redeemer from the little town of Bethlehem in 5:2 (which has already come true) and the vision of the New World under the Redeemer's reign in 4:1-4, when swords will be beaten to ploughshares and spears into pruning hooks, and every man and woman sits under their own vine and fig tree, and none shall make them afraid.

Micah's ministry as a prophet was during the reigns of kings Jotham, Ahaz and Hezekiah, a span of some 61 years in Judah (At this time the kingdom had split into two: Judah and Israel.) Sometime during the reigns of the three kings, Israel was severely beaten and taken over by Assyria. Its people were exiled to Assyria, and even Judah was overrun by Assyrian troops. And though Jerusalem, the capital city was not taken, King Hezekiah was heavily fined by the invaders until Hezekiah asked for God's help.

Despite the general picture of war and political subjection, Micah lived in a period of economic revolution. As it happens today, material prosperity had spawned selfish materialism brought about by political alliances especially among national leaders. Religion became a means of achieving human desires. Personal and social values disintegrated. Wealth was invested in land with the result that the traditional system of agricultural small holdings collapsed with the growth of vast estates. Material and emotional distress ensued. Even religious leaders could do no more than echo the spirit of the period, supporting the society that gave them their livelihood.

To this materially developing society, Micah spoke. He became the social commentator of his day, the social conscience of a society whose leaders had become quite enamored by their new wealth, high positions and new friends of influence, and had forgotten their responsibilities as national leaders.

Unlike other minor prophets such as Amos and Joel who had much to say to the idolatry and immorality rampant in Israel and Judah due to the pagan

Canaanite religion, Micah confined his utterances to the problems arising from the social injustices perpetuated upon the small landowners, farmers and peasants. His condemnation was scathing:

"Woe to those who plan iniquity,
to those who plot evil on their beds!
At morning's light they carry it out
because it is in their power to do it.
They covet fields and seize them,
and houses, and take them.
They defraud a man of his home,
a fellowman of his inheritance."
Micah 2:1-2

Why did he focus on the issue of landgrabbing? For two reasons:

First, because Micah knew what he was talking about. He came from the southwest area of Judah. It was a plain of fertile land owned by small farmers, and had become the envy of land investors and the nouveaux riches of his time. He saw for himself how the little people were victimized—if they were not fooled or cajoled to sell their lands, they were threatened with harm or even killed. It happened then, it happens now.

Second, because Micah believed that true faithfulness to God could not be shown by rituals and religiosity but by doing justice, loving kindness and walking humbly with God (cf. 6:6-8).

Questions for Discussion

1. Do you know of anyone today claiming to be a "prophet"? Comparing

with what we know of Micah so far, how is that 'prophet' different from him?

2. In terms of social justice (or lack of it), how is your world today different from that ofMicah's time? In what way is it similar?

3. What social injustices do you find in your family? In your community? In our country? How is the land situation in the country in relation to development and globalization?

4. In the face of these injustices, are you (as an individual, group or church) using opportunities to respond in the same way as Micah? Why or why not?

Comments on the Text (Part 2)

Micah's Message (3:1-18)

The true prophets of biblical times did not mince words. Not that it was not dangerous. Elijah had to run for his life, Amos endured banishment, Jeremiah was imprisoned and John the Baptist literally lost his head. Nevertheless, truth had to be spoken. And Micah was for truth.

His message was addressed to three groups of people in Judah—all of them in positions of national leadership. His messages or oracles all revolved on "justice" (3: 1, 8-9).

First, he spoke against the national leaders: to the "heads of Jacob, rulers of the house of Israel" (3:1). These are primarily the court offcials, especially in their role as guardians ofjustice. Their equivalent today would be those in our judiciary, the interpreters and dispensers of the law. What had they done?

The supposed guardians of justice had distorted their functions. Their ethical standards were turned upside down. According to Micah, they hated good and loved evil (v.2). These strong emotional words of "hate" and "love" were the very same words used by Amos, the prophet who came before Micah, in his own appeal to the people of Judah. "Hate evil and love good, maintain justice in the courts," he said (Amos 5:15). Isaiah spoke in the same vein: "Stop doing wrong; learn to do right!" (Isaiah 1:16b-17a).

Corruption in the courts was so bad. Micah pictured the court officials as cannibalistic savages—tearing off their victims' skin, eating their flesh, breaking their bones, and chopping them up for the boiling pot. There was in short, legal and moral cannibalism. Instead of promoting the all-time moral and social code from God handed down to them through Moses, these offcials replaced it with their own arbitrary rules. They favored the well-off, and deprived the poor of the little they had. And in the process, the judges got fat from the alliance that they had forged with the rich.

But according to Micah these fat judges who winked at bribes, and threw poor litigants out of their courts would also have their day. Tit for tat, God, the ultimate arbiter of justice would turn against them, be deaf to their cries and would not be there in their time of need. The very treatment they afforded the poor they would get by divine fiat, and no mercy will be given them.

Second, Micah was not sparing of his own colleagues (3: 5-8). Earlier we said the prophetic ministry was an honorable institution. But like any other institution, its members could dishonor it by being unfaithful to their high calling. Micah must have been embarrassed by his colleagues' spiritually-polluting behavior. In turn, he must have been a great embarrassment to them too, if not an outright pain in the neck. He cramped their style, so to speak. What were they doing?

Apparently, Micah's colleagues had developed the fine art of what we may call today "envelopmental prophecy,"* that is, they had learned to match their divine messages for fees proportionate to their customer's pockets. (*The term describes the phenomenon in the Philippines where some journalists receive money (put in an envelope) from interested parties to write favorable news about them. It is called "envelopmental joumalism.")

To these prophets, God no longer figured in their counsel and advice. The content of their oracles was no longer dictated by what God had to say but on the kind of clients who came to them. Prophesying had become a lucrative business. The rich did not have to make diffcult choices anymore. When the elite consulted the prophets on decisions they had to make, the prophets would say to them, "Great plan, go ahead. Peace!" Or, "Excellent move, carry on. God is with you!" Thus, for a price, they dispensed shallow optimism. But to the poor man who had nothing to give, they foretold for him a bleak future, and drove him away for wasting their time.

The lightheartedness with which the prophets took God's word in Micah's time was also expressed by Jeremiah many generations after:

"From the least to the greatest,
all are greedy for gain;
prophets andpriests alike,
all practice deceit.
They dress the wound ofmy people
as though it were not serious.
'Peace, peace' they say,
when there is no peace."

Jeremiah 6:13-14

Their punishment would be most tragic: the removal of the gift of prophecy. A day would come when they would be in search of God's message, but there would be none. They would seek for God's light, but there would only be silence and darkness. Tampering with God's gift to us only invites disaster and uselessness.

At this point, the religious leaders must have been not only irked by Micah's gadflying; they must have been livid with self-righteous indignation? "Who are you, Micah, anyway? Get off your high horse and show us your credentials!" they must have demanded. Unlike them, Micah could declare:

> *"But as for me, I am filled with power,*
> *with the Spirit of the Lord,*
> *and with justice and might,*
> *to declare to Jacob his transgression,*
> *to Israel his sin."* (v.8)

He was saying that he was not really a courageous man, except that he was granted power from on high to say the truth. It was not he, but the Spirit of the Lord consuming his soul. His God-given sense of justice was violated by the unconscionable behavior of his colleagues against the weak and the poor. And for him to remain silent was to be unfaithful to God. His primary concern was justice, thus his appeal was to their moral conscience. To encourage right and discourage wrong was his only motive. He had no interest to protect, and he was risking his own life.

Here in a nutshell is set the important qualifications for a true prophet of any age and time: his center is God, his orientation is towards truth, his message is grounded in reality. He has no vested interest: only to promote justice and righteousness.

Having established his claims, Micah proceeded to speak against the third group (3:9-12). Here, "rulers of the house of Jacob and chiefs of the house of Israel" (NRSV) refer to the wider group who made up the establishment rather than just the court officials in the beginning verses.

In Isaiah 3 is a list of men of influence in the capital and in the country. These were the professional soldiers, the army captains and generals, judges and prophets, diviners and elders, aristocrats and counselors, sorcerers and soothsayers. The last two are believed to be influences from the East (Isaiah 2:6). As members of the Judean establishment, they held in their hands the reins of society. They were the elite, the power-holders.

Tragically, the very same influential people had an abhorrence ofjustice; they twisted everything straight, according to Micah. How?

They put up infrastructures at the cost of people's lives. How was this done? Jeremiah gave a glimpse of the oppression, if we fast forward a century later, when the prophet attacked the building frenzy of king Jehoiakim (Jeremiah 22:13-14, 17).

> *"Woe to him who builds his palace by unrighteousness,*
> *his upper rooms by injustice,*
> *making his countrymen work for nothing,*
> *not paying them for their labor.*
> *He says, 'I will build myself a great palace*
> *with spacious upper rooms. '*
> *So he makes large windows in it*
> *panels it with cedar*
> *and decorates it in red...*
>
> *...But your eyes and your heart*
> *are set only on dishonest gain,*
> *on shedding innocent blood*
> *and on oppression and extortion."*

Back to Micah's day, similar evils were happening: court officials handed down judgment for a fee; priests gave religious instruction for monetary consideration; prophets divined for money, while everybody was paying lip service to God and quoting his words to rationalize their actions.

The punishment was grim. Not only was the whole establishment to be destroyed but the whole nation would suffer. The ways of the 'corrupt leaders of the land had been institutionalized; it had seeped into the systems and structures of society. Nothing could remove it except exile and banishment. Micah's prediction came true long after he had died.

Micah's hope

In Micah's world, there was going to be a silver lining behind the bleakness of his day. He spoke of the last days where the social ills he enumerated earlier would be no more. The implements of war and oppression would be turned into instruments of peace and abundance. The picture was that of agricultural peace because the issue he had to contend with was agricultural in nature. Today, the roots of much of the injustice among the 21st century developing societies is still the land. In Micah's vision, the Lord himself *"shall judge among many people, and rebuke strong nations afar off..."* (4:3a, Thompson Bible).

To be the conscience of society is also to be ambassadors of hope. Evil leaders, immoral courts, compromising religious offcials, wicked structures and systems are not forever. God may allow them to exist for a time, but judgment will come to fulfill the demands of justice. God has the last word. To the oppressor, it is judgment; to the oppressed, it is salvation.

Wherever we go as today's prophets, let us keep the hope in our hearts and broadcast it abroad. Both sides of the world need it.

Questions for Discussion

1. What are the equivalent groups in our nation today that correspond to the three groups addressed by Micah? What do they share in common? What are their differences?

2. What forms of corruption, oppression, or injustice are you aware of in your church? community? country? How do you react to these? In what ways can you be like Micah? List them down. Which of these can you do alone, and which with others of the same mind?

3. John Stott says the days of original prophets are past. But we can be "secondary prophets," that is, we can be women and men who bring the Word of God into situations of social ill and wrongdoing in our community and/or country. Like Micah, we can serve as moral and social conscience. What do you think would this require from you?

4. From the lives of biblical prophets, we may glean three important qualities that a prophet should have. First, he/she must be an astute student of the Word. A prophet is a man/woman of the Word of God. Every action, every issue, every program must go through the test of Scriptures—studied carefully with an open mind (and ideally with others), evaluated in prayerful obedience, and embraced as the basis of our action. This is the distinctive of a Christian social activist, the prophet of today.

Question: How do you read the Bible? Have you ever considered your Bible as the basis ofyour social action and involvement in society as well, not only a source for personal spiritual uplift?

Second, to become "modern-day prophets" we need to have our ears to the ground. We should not only be aware of the dynamics of our society, but also be keenly interested in how social realities affect people and be sensitive as to how the teachings of the Scriptures impinge on these realities. Coupled with the expansion of our social awareness is the refinement of our social analysis. Developing the ability to read the times correctly is both a gift from God and a result of careful study. The men of Issachar had this ability: *"...they understood the times and knew what Israel should do."* (1 Chronicles 12:32)

Question: How do you think could you develop this social and biblical sensibility?

Third, because the Word has a bearing on our social situation, as modern-day prophets we need to articulate and/or demonstrate our discoveries appealing to reason, to morality and to reality as Micah did. To be sure, this is not an easy task, but a valid and biblical Christian response which we pray that more believers would engage in. In our world today, the cause of justice is minimally addressed while corruption and oppression in high places prevail. The weak and the poor remain generally voiceless.

Question: Are you willing to be a voice of the poor? Would you help them find their own voice?

The Text in Our Context

Below is a radio editorial that illustrates modem-day 'prophesying.'

"OF DAMS AND DEVELOPMENT"

A war against the construction of huge dams is a-brewing worldwide. An international day of mass action against dams is shaping up. About 30 million people is set to simultaneously join the protest, according to the International Rivers Network (IRN), an organization coordinating the mass action. "This is to point out that the issues on dam-building is not only local but global as well," says Aleta Brown, campaign associate of IRN.

Why would people be against dams, we may ask? Don't dams harness the scattered water sources and provide efficient water supply to our fields, homes and factories? Don't they generate electricity to light up our streets and run the engines of our industries? Aren't dams harbingers of what we fondly call 'development'?

At first glance they are. The opposition, however, stems from the fact that the construction of huge dams results in massive environmental destruction and displacement ofpeople. Thirty to sixty million people, especially cultural communities, have been reportedly displaced by large dam projects.

We need not go out of our country to support this report. The displacement of thousands of our countrymen as a result of the construction of the Angat dam, for example, and the violence and death it sowed among our people make us hesitant to hail it as a channel of our progress.

Today, concerned groups including the Ibaloi, an indigenous group in Pangasinan, are appealing to our government to listen to the plea of the residents of San Roque and San Manuel, Pangasinafi, the project site of San Roque dam. Bishop Allan Ray Sarte of the United Church ofChrist in San Manuel stands behind the dam protesters.

His main concem is to find out whether, indeed, the govemment has the capability to resettle the thousands ofpeople who will be displaced by the project. On the other hand, the Ibalois claim that the project site is part oftheir ancestral land.

Conventional wisdom says we've got to pay the price of progress. That is fair enough. But we need to ask again: For how much and at what cost? We believe that dam construction companies and the government need to be more humane, culturally-sensitive, and respectful of the people's fears and needs. We need to remember that our place, our home, our personhood are important components of development; not massive cement walls, turbines or impressive catch basins, however wide and however long.

The human element is a basic equation in any development, be it a fly-over or a dam. The person is the very reason why all these development efforts are done in the first place. Why, then be indifferent to reason? Or worse, why eradicate the person?

(*Courage to Live These Days*, QC: Institute for Studies in Asian Church and Culture, 1999, p.66)

Question: In what way is this radio editorial a prophetic voice? List down modern ways in which Christians can be prophets of their times.

Social Injustice Depicted in Song: An Artistic Model

In the oppressed silence of the poor,
the poet singer or the artist becomes their voice.
To be a voice to the voiceless is a basic responsibility
of all Christians regardless of position and gifting in life.

Text

PSALM 10

1 Why, O Lord, do you stand far off?
Why do you hide yourself in times of trouble?
2 In his arrogance the wicked man hunts down the weak,
who are caught in the schemes he devises.
3 He boast of the cravings of his heart;
he blesses the greedy and reviles the Lord.
4 In his pride the wicked does not seek him;
in all his thoughts there is no room for God.
5 His ways are always prosperous;
he is haughty and your laws are far from him;
he sneers at all his enemies.
6 He says to himself, "Nothing will shake me;
I'll always be happy and never have trouble."

7 His mouth is full of curses and lies and threats;
trouble and evil are under his tongue.
8 He lies in wait near the villages;
from ambush he murders the innocent,

watching in secret for his victims.
9He lies in wait like a lion in cover;
he lies in wait to catch the helpless;
he catches the helpless and drags them off in his net.
10His victims are crushed, they collapse;
they fall under his strength.
11He says to himself, "God has forgotten;
he covers his face and never sees.

12Arise, Lord! Lift up your hand, O God.
Do not forget the helpless.
13Why does the wicked man revile God?
Why does he say to himself,
"He won't call me to account"?
14But you, O God, do see trouble and grief;
you consider it to take it in hand.
The victim commits himself to you;
you are the helper of the fatherless.
15Break the arm of the wicked and evil man;
call him to account for his wickedness that would not be found out.

16The Lord is King forever and ever;
the nations will perish from his land.
17You hear, O Lord, the desire of the afflicted;
you encourage them, and you listen to their cry,
18defending the fatherless and the oppressed,
in order that man, who is of the earth,
may terrify no more.

Questions on the Text

1. As a psalm to be sung in a congregational gathering in the Temple, why would this particular song be jarring? Comforting? Hopeful?

2. This particular psalm is classified among the lament psalms. What is the singer lamenting about?

3. How does the singer describe the wicked man in terms of the state of his heart and mind, his actions, his words and life? (vv. 2-11)

4. In the face of such a man, the seeming irreverent tone of the singer (v.1) towards God changes in vv. 12-18. Describe the change. How does he regard God now in relation to the wicked, his victims, the world and himself?

5. Taking the song as a whole, what is the singer's basic view of life?
Is using art (in the case here, a song) a legitimate way to address social issues in society? Why or why not?

6. Is there a case of injustice, oppression and victimization happening in your neighborhood, community and society today? How would you respond to it in an artistic way?

Comments on the Text

Gary Granada is a Christian artist who has won a number of national awards in the music industry. He is a composer, singer, arranger and a fine guitarist. In many song contests, while most singers would write about love, Gary would often write on themes that certainly disturb the peace ofthe comfortable and powerful. One of his winning pieces has the prosaic title "Bahay" (House).

Filipinos, or Third World citizens anywhere could not listen to the song without getting a lump in their throats if not a tear in their eyes. For instance, after Gary sang the song at the 1989 Lausanne Congress in Manila, an indescribable hush descended upon some 5000 international participants, not a few misty-eyed before they erupted into a long applause. Everyone knew the song was not only to entertain but to stir up a Christian conscience towards the reality of slum-dwellers in all developing countries, derisively called "squatters." Their ever-growing presence in highly urbanized cities and towns ofthe world dramatizes the yawning gap between the rich and the poor, and the many social ills it spawns. And indeed, institutions like government, school and church have often neglected their plight, if not exploited their vulnerability, letting their tilting shanties pass off as "houses" for human dwelling.

Most of the psalms in Holy Scriptures are like Gary's songs. They disturb and jar us from our complacent perch. In fact, the largest category of the psalms fall under songs of lament. And often, these psalms are against the oppression of the weak and needy, the lack of justice, the seeming triumph of evil in the world, the neglect of widows and orphans, the failure of leaders to protect their people from their enemies. Psalm 10:1-18 is an example of how a song, a religious song could become a fitting response to the social inequities in our world today from a poet-singer.

Taken as is (for some scholars think that Psalm 10 used to be part of Psalm 9), the song erupts peeved, impatient and almost angry accusing God of his seeming indifference and absence (v.1) in the midst of a disorderly world. Evil men appear to have the run of society but suffer no harm. The psalmist wails a long "why?" His sensitivity to social ills and his strong belief that God has the prerogative over all of life drove him to ask at the risk of being irreverent. But the poet-singer is not the only person in the Bible to ask God "why?" Early on, someone did (Psalm 2:1). Others like Moses, Elijah and Job, at some point in their lives, confronted God with the same question.

Often Christians today who are sensitive to social disparities cannot help but sometimes ask God similarly. The ethnic conflicts that have killed thousands, the ideological wars that have annihilated millions, AIDS, worldwide famine, the prostitution and slavery of children and women as a result of the imperious, unfeeling and greedy way world commerce is pursued make us wonder whether, indeed, God is interested in the affairs of people.

The song may have begun in a note of despair, exasperation or irreverence, but the singer rights himself up at the end. His plaint has a basis.

Now, his lyre takes the listener to a reality in life of two kinds of people inhabiting the world: the wicked or "the man of earth," and the hapless poor. The wicked struts about boasting of what he is capable of doing. He dismisses God as a figment of a weakling's imagination (vv.3-4), and he seems to be right.

Without soliciting divine help, the wicked gets on with life in style. He is prosperous and powerful, and quite certain in his mind that his whole life and his descendants would always be secure and remain untouched by poverty, or any other disaster (vv. 5-6).

Where does his security lie? From foulness. His mind is polluted with evil plans and oppression against others, and his language reeks with curses, lies and deceit. His power comes from wounding and trampling the hapless, the poor, the fatherless and the oppressed (vv. 7-10) Yet, for all these, he thrives.

In many places today, wickedness is palpable. It is lodged in certain personalities we can easily identify. The corrupt politicians, profit-hungry businesspersons, bribable judges, abusive police officers, powerful landlords and landgrabbers, crime/drug syndicates, criminals, racist groups, wife batterers, and the toughie down the street are wickedness personified. But wickedness as we have observed in reality are more than evil people sowing evil deeds. Wickedness can lodge in institutions that push for laws and policies that wring the poor of their rights to a secure life. Or, they could be ideologies and/or systems that promote discrimination of race, gender, economic, social, religious or political status. Or they could be structures that inherently divide the powerful and the weak, the rich and the poor in society. And once wicked men have systematized their wickedness, evil becomes faceless and amorphous; therefore, it is harder to identify and fight.

For how could the poor fight? They only bow in silence (v. 10). Unintended or not, the situation of the poor begs for description in this passage. The psalmist devotes 9 or 10 verses to describe the wicked, but for the poor there are none at all. They are crushed, they sink down, and fall without even uttering a word.

It takes artistic genius for this poet-singer to depict the plight of the poor in the structure of his song by means of omission. For in the face of violence and power, the poor can only be silent. Survival comes in meekly surrendering.

With this their utter helplessness, the psalmist bursts into a plea for God to arise declaring that God, after all, is not a neglectful or absent God. He *"sees trouble and grief"* (v. 14), the helper of the fatherless. He has the power to break the arm of the wicked for unlike the puny boasting of the wicked, God the Lord is *"king forever and ever."* (v. 16) His prayer-song to God on behalf of the poor is both precise and hopeful:

> 17*You hear, O Lord, the desire of the afflicted;*
> *you encourage them, and you listen to their cry,*
> 18*defending the fatherless and the oppressed,*
> *in order that man, who is of the earth,*
> *may terrify no more.* (vv. 17-18)

And with this, the psalmist ends his song.

Questions for Discussion

1. How is the situation as sung by the poet-singer still true today? Cite specific events or situations?

2. The prayer-song maybe addressed to God, but it is sung by a worshipping congregation. What could be its effect on the people worshipping? How could it possibly advance the cause of justice among them and in the world?

3. What other art forms can Christian artists utilize to address social realities biblically? Can you engage in any of them? If not, do you know of anyone whom you can encourage?

4. What is the role of Christian artists in society today?

The Text in our Context

The artist as a voice for the poor

In the oppressed silence of the poor, the poet-singer or the artist becomes their voice. To be a voice of the voiceless is a basic responsibility of all Christians regardless of position and gifting in life.

> *"Speak up for those who cannot speak for themselves,*
> *for the rights of all who are destitute.*
> *Speak up and judge fairly;*
> *defend the rights of the poor and needy."*
> Proverbs 31:8-9

This is not only an advice given by an insightful mother to his son who is a leader, but something Christian artists can also take to heart.

The Holy Scriptures is replete with artistry, and in many biblical episodes art forms were used to promote justice and righteousness. Nathan had only to tell a story to bring deep conviction to the sinning King David (2 Samuel 12:17). The prophet Isaiah made use of dramatic portrayals to stir up the conscience of the Jewish nation. Jesus used parables depicting economic and social conditions, and the letter of James pointedly addresses social discrimination within the church, and the wider issue of rich-poor relations.

History equally has shown how art has stoked the fire of social revolutions. ***Uncle Tom's Cabin*** written in 1851 is an anti-slavery novel by Harriet Elizabeth Beecher Stowe. In the process of recreating characters, scenes, and incidents with humor and realism, Stowe also analyzed the issue of slavery in midwest New England, USA, and in the south during the days of the Fugitive Slave Law. The book is believed to have intensified the rift between the north and the south over slavery which eventually led to the Civil War.

Around the same time, an English writer was tackling similar social themes in his novels in England. Charles Dickens did not only write highly entertaining stories about life in his country, but his stories exposed the ugly underside of the industrial revolution. For example, his stories revolved around underworld criminals, child labor and the mistreatment of the poor in ***Oliver Twist***, the wasteful and cruel legal process, neglect of the poor, false humanitarianism and poor sanitation in his long novel, ***Bleak House*** and the evils of materialism, utilitarianism and government inefficiency in ***Little Dorrit***.

Jose Mercado Rizal used art to advance the cause of freedom in our country. His two socially subversive novels, ***Noli me Tangere*** and ***El Filibusterismo*** helped awaken the Filipinos' aspiration for dignity and liberty. The ***Noli*** on the one hand, exposed the moral bankruptcy of the Catholic friars and the oppression, injustice and cruelty of Spanish rule. ***El Filibusterismo***, on the other hand, tantalizingly toyed with the idea of revolution against the colonial masters. Both novels were banned during the Spanish regime. For being true to himself, to his country and his art, Jose Rizal was executed as a traitor to Spain, but today he is a hero to the Filipino people. His example remains a challenge to all freedom-loving citizens of the world.

Necessarily however, when an artist voices the plight of the weak and the disadvantaged, he is not out to usurp their right to speak and act for themselves. Rather in articulating the pain and longing of the poor, his purpose is to awaken their sense of right and dignity, strengthen their hope in God, and empower them to express the longings in their hearts. Over and over again the poet-singers in the Psalms repeat the timeless truth that God does save and cares for them.

> *"For he will deliver the needy who cry out,*
> *the afflicted who have no one to help.*
> *He will take pity on the weak and the needy*
> *and save the needy from death.*
> *He will rescue them from oppression and violence,*
> *for precious is their blood in his sight."*
>
> Psalm 72: 12-14

And as for Gary, his song "Bahay" lives on. It is sung in the hovels clinging precariously on river banks, on the stretch ofwalls holding back Manila Bay and in the art cafes of the socially-aware elite of Metro Manila. It goes this way:

Isang araw ako 'y nadalaw sa bahay tambakan
Labin limang mag-anak ang duo'y nagsiksikan
Nagtitiis sa munting barung-barong na sira-sira
Habang doon sa isang mansion halos walang nakatira

(One day I visited a "house" in the garbage damp
Squeezed inside was a household of fifteen people
Enduring a small, make-shift, broken down shanty
While a nearby mansion was almost empty.)

Sa init ng tabla't karton, sila doo'y nakakulong
Sa lilim ng yerong kalawang at mga sirang gulong
Pinagtagpi-tagping basurang pinatungan ng bato
Hindi ko maintindihan bakit ang tawag sa ganito ay bahay.

(Imprisoned inside wooden slabs and corrupted boxes
Shaded by rusting zinc sheets and worn-out tires
Mended together by scraps of trash and held down by stones
I could not understand why such a thing is called a house.)

Sinulat ko ang nakita ng aking mga mata

Ang kanilang kalagayan ginawan ko ng kanta
Iginuhit at isinalarawan ang naramdamgn
At sinangguni ko sa mga taong marami ang alam

(I decided to write a story about what my eyes saw
And even made a song that others may hear and know
I painted what I felt and put up a simple play
And asked knowledgeable people what they can say.)

Isang bantog na senador ang unang nilapitan ko
At dalubhasang propesor ng malaking kolehiyo
Ang pinagpala sa mundo, ang diyaryo at ang pulpito
Lahat sila'y nagkasundo na ang tawag sa ganito ay bahay.

(A famous senator was the first person I came to see
And then an expert professor of a prominent university
And a blessed businessman, and a newsman and a churchman
And they all agreed that indeed it was a house.)

Maghapo't magdamag silang kakayod, kakahig
Pagdaka'y tutukang nakaupo lang sa sahig
Sa papag na gutay-gutay ay pipiliting hihimlay
Di hamak na mainam pa ang pahingahan ng mga patay

(Day and night they scrape the mountain of trash
And eat like chickens on the ground as they squat
And then force their bodies to sleep on an old torn bed
Far, far better is the resting place of a rich man's dead.)

Baka naman isang araw kayo doon ay maligaw
Mahipo n'yo at marinig at maamoy at matanaw
Hindi ako nangungutya kayo na rin ang magpasya
Sa palagay ninyo kaya, ito sa mata ng Maylikha ay bahay?

(But if one day you get lost and find yourself in such a place
And feel and hear and smell and see them face to face
I neither scorn nor deride, I leave it up to you, you decide
Would you think that in the eyes of the Creator it is a house?)

1. Have you read/seen/experienced an art form that has stirred up your social conscience lately? Relate how it has affected you and why?

2. Examine how art is used in your work or ministry. What is its impact on your work? If you have not utilized any art form, would you be willing to explore the possibility? List down ways of how you could go about using an art form in your work/ministry.

The New Urban Village & Its Challenge to the Church

4

Michael A. Mata

Aristotle is credited with saying "A city consists of differing kinds of humans; similar humans do not bring about a city."

As the world's urban populations grow, cities become spaces where increasingly diverse peoples negotiate such differences as language, citizenship, ethnicity and race, class and wealth, and gender (Kihato et al., 2010). The New Urban Agenda acknowledges that while cultural diversity can pose a variety of challenges it can also bring significant social, economic, and cultural contributions to urban life (UN Habitat, 2016). The term "diversity" has a variety of meanings in the urban literature. Among urban designers it refers to intermingling building types; among city planners it means mixed uses or class and racial-ethnic heterogeneity; for sociologists and cultural analysts it emphasizes the latter meaning. Some writers on the urban context focus on only one of these interpretations; many, however, see each type of diversity as linked to the others, even while there is disagreement as to the direction of causality.

One need not spend time in distilling interpretations to get a glimpse of what multicultural diversity looks like in our urban world. Simply join the flow of pedestrian traffic of any central district of a major urban city, or stroll down a renovated commercial strip of an expanding city, and chances are you will encounter the new urban world. Whether it is Nairobi, Toronto, Singapore, London, Los Angeles, or Sydney you will quickly come upon the sights, smells and sounds of international communities engaging in economic and cultural activities. You will see signs promoting local services or imported goods catering to particular ethnic groups; financial institutions carrying unfamiliar names from distant countries and gathering places identified by non-native languages; family-owned businesses and new enterprises. The scene is no longer of the exotic or pop-up because these people are now interwoven into the social fabric of the local community. Their children attend local schools, they pay taxes and use local medical and social services. Unlike the immigrants before them, they interact with their homeland and new land in more profound and dynamic ways. These multicultural expressions of local community reflect powerful forces at play on the global scale (Sandercock, 2013). These forces are driving the evolution of a new urban reality and in turn raise provocative questions about the mission of the church in the urban age.

The New City

At the dawn of the new millennium humanity achieved a demographic milestone. For the first time in history, more people were counted as living in cities than in rural areas; first and second generation immigrants are no longer a minority. Explosive population growth and a torrent of migration from the countryside are creating cities that dwarf the great capitals of the past. In the early 1990s people across the globe were moving to the cities at a rate of over 200,000 per day, nearly 75 million people each year. The pace has picked up and the urban population is expected to grow in the next few decades to some 6.4 billion by 2050

(UN, 2014). Most of the growth will be in the majority world, including some of the poorest countries on the planet.

The migration of people from the country to the city and from foreign lands to new lands, is not a new story. However, the conventional explanation of the "push" of poverty and the "pull" of economic opportunity does not fully explain the current level of movement. Neither poverty, overpopulation, nor economic stagnation in themselves serve to trigger mass movement, although they obviously play a significant role. A natural catastrophe will generate movement but it is temporal. Without doubt, wars, religious conflict and political repression fuel mobility patterns. However, in the past 25 years or so the prime factor in the movement of vast numbers of people has been the allure of contemporary urban life with its promised economic opportunities and material amenities.

Since the founding of the first city, cities have been at the hub of all important activity, shaping the political, intellectual and moral character of our societies. They are the centers of communication, commerce, creativity and cultural life. However, the radical technological and economic changes of the last quarter century have transformed cities into vital links of a highly interconnected global village (Khanna, 2016). With this global transformation has come the emergence of a new cultural perspective that is decidedly urban, Western and consumption-oriented — forever shaping the consciousness of the village's inhabitants and challenging our notion of "urban."

Globalization

Cultural invasion is also nothing new. It has been with us at least since Alexander the Great spread Greek culture from the Nile to the Ganges. Where new ideas once advanced at the foot pace of advancing armies or merchants' caravans, they are now spread instantly by satellites bringing Hollywood's fantasies and Madison Avenue's commercials to places as widely separated and isolated as the Alaskan tundra, Guatemalan villages,

Kenyan bush and Andean mountains. It has been said that the formation of culture is the process of the telling of stories. Today's far-reaching signals have new tales to tell of affluence, freedom and power.

The acceleration of information technology has facilitated the promotion of these new stories and retelling of stories (Castells, 1998). Throughout the village people are using the same electronic devices to watch or listen to the same commercially produced songs, stories, and soap operas, in the same instant of real time. Alaskan children watch Teletubbies cartoons. "Baywatch" is popular in many Arab countries (and elsewhere), even as viewers from the Muslim community compare its glamour and turmoil with their conservative family-centered culture. Traditional ways of life are challenged under the spell of advanced communication technologies. At one time films, television, radio, periodicals, clothing, games, toys, and theme parks were the media for disseminating Western ideas, international images and spreading global dreams. And now the world wide web has shrunk the globe to human scale; cyberspace has created new nodes of connections and exchange at nanosecond speed.

Indeed, these transformations take place almost invisibly, without the conscious decisions of the people affected. Even under repressive governments, which have proven ineffectual in curtailing the flow of information, nearly all sectors of the village are subject to what can be called "cultural synchronization" or as it is more commonly called "globalization." This homogenization of the global village according to Western commercial cultural patterns is driven by urbanization and reinforced by innovations in telecommunications.

Due to the global commodification of Western cultural cities, for example New York, LosAngeles, London, Paris, and Berlin have all become worldwide symbols of the good life. Both well-advertised and underground travel routes have turned far away cities into magnets for millions of people who leave their homelands in search of the more glamorous and exciting life they have seen on the screen or heard in the beat of a song played on the radio or downloaded off the internet.

Exegeting the New Urban Landscape

These urban or global processes are visible in the built landscape. There exist within the spatial dimension of our global village, our cities, clear signs of the emerging (postmodern?) urban reality. All sorts of factors--demographic, economic, ecological, theological and so on--interweave to form the living, vibrant and imperfect miniature world that is a city. In turn, all of these dynamic variables interact with and are affected by its built substance: some of it is beautiful and good to be in, some exacerbate the struggle to be human. But this interplay contributes to the creation of new patterns of social life and interaction. The "city" is the text, or guide, to what is happening on a global scale.

At first glance, the city can be overwhelming in its complexity reflected in its design and structure. Yet, on closer examination we find that the values, hopes, ideals, beliefs of the emerging new multicultural urban world are expressed explicitly and distinctively in the physical landscape itself. Architectural style has as much to say about the promotion of certain values and cultural perspectives as it has about the role and function of the structure itself.

To be sure, urban form is never devoid of social content: it is merely the grid within which we organize our daily lives. People give life to the city, they embody culture and they express it in novel and creative ways. If there is one distinct feature of this social dimension of the emerging urban reality, it is the increasing diversity of the city's residents. Immigration adds ethnic diversity and continues to create ethnic enclaves. Regional migration creates geographic subcultures, and divisions along color lines reinforce their own kind of diversity. Communities forged along lines of generational or sexual preferences have emerged and will continue to make their place.

All people, all parts of society, seek to build new lives for themselves. In erecting or reconfiguring structures in which to work, live and play, they are building communities in a way that will give themselves and their families a sense of permanence and sustainability. A great deal is invested in place-making, and the outcome is a city teeming with life and often unconsciously searching for expressions of something more transcendent. As such the creativity, color, brightness, and vibrancy of life that is found in the city take on kaleidoscopic dimensions that reverberate throughout the urban landscape.

As mentioned earlier, looking at and into corner shops or neighborhood shopping malls can reveal the cosmopolitan character of the evolving city. They are places which cater to the material needs and desires of their customers. Attractive, intriguing, descriptive window displays and outside signage not only advertise what products are being sold but who would most likely frequent a particular shop. Koreans have transformed neighborhoods into their own likeness in Los Angeles just as Indians and Pakistanis have in London. Immigrants from Asia have established colonies in all the major cities. Indeed, this hypermobility has been a huge factor in the creation of a world with permeable borders (Schiller & Caglar, 2008).

Whether they come to the city from across the ocean or state border, there are global dreams at stake. The migrants bring dreams and visions not only for themselves but their children and their children's children. Some of these hopes are fulfilled and others shattered. In the day-to-day experience of life, the struggles and the pains of life are ever present and so much a part of the landscape of the familiar that we function in life as though they do not exist. (Often, we literally walk pass the very clues that reveal the failed aspirations of our new neighbor or local merchant.) These aspirations are not only conveyed in their demeanor, attire, attitudes, and the manner in which they interact with others but most significantly they stamp these ideas (i.e. themselves) into the surrounding terrain. The color of paint chosen for the house, the kind of vegetation planted in the garden, the religious artifacts in the windows can all provide clues about the hopes and desires (as well as the ethnic identity and income level) of those who live or work in a particular neighborhood or cluster of buildings.

To be sure, the struggle to sustain life, even if that is just survival, takes on a creative but disparate edge in our new world. The presence of the consummate recyclers, picking up debris left in public places and rummaging through private garbage, reminds us that not all have found what they had hoped to find in the city. Nonetheless, our streets and parks would be a great deal messier and our landfills overflowing if they did not pick up after us and help us take care of our garbage. The sex worker on the corner or the lines outside a Blood Plasma Center reminds us that when legitimate and respectable, or at least acceptable, avenues of maintaining life are limited or non- existent, people find other ways of generating the means to sustain themselves. Increasingly scenes like these and others will not be restricted to certain "parts of town." This is our world today, struggling, in conflict, divided, where people find themselves lining up on one side of the prosperity / poverty fence, with most on the poverty side. Thus, those without the means, the access or the prestige are more and more finding themselves vulnerable to the negative effects of the rapidly changing world. They comprise the "new urban poor," working individuals or families without the sustainable income to provide for the basic needs.

At the end of the 20th century, a new so-called suburban underclass emerged where the permanently poor live in the midst of plenty (Suburbs and Areas and the New American Poverty, 2015). Wherever there are new housing tracks or office buildings there will be toilets to clean and lawns to maintain and those willing to accept meager wages to do so. Experiences such as this point out that the old questions about God and Mammon, wealth and injustice, development and stewardship, undoubtedly, will resurface even more vigorously in the 21st Century.

Back to the Future

In the Constantinian era, Christianity furnished the overarching world view and moral ethos for Western civilization. This is not to say that Christians always practiced well what they preached, but rather that a

"Christian world view" dominated, at least in Western society as it had no real competitors.

The Constantinian age of Christendom ended at some point in time (For many the modern age is also coming to a close). The Church now finds itself in a situation more like its pre-Constantinian experience, in a pre-Christian or post-Christian era. And this means, as theologian Harvey Cox suggests, we probably have more to learn from those who were agitated by Christendom than from those who found it comfortable. (Cox, 1984).

There was a time when virtually all our European and American ancestors and missionaries could imagine no substitute for the church. Certainly, traditional and established Judeo-Christian forms of religion are still very present in the landscape and their places of worship remain impressive in their architectural style. However, the activities inside are increasingly disappointing in appeal to the new generation and often disconnected from the change around them. Yet, contrary to the predictions of social scientists, the urban terrain testifies that religion is alive and well in the emerging urban world. If not in the mainstream certainly on the spiritual periphery.

While historic forms of religion continue to attend to the spiritual needs of their constituencies they now have to be understood in relation to a host of different and evolving religious expressions. As people move to a new land or city they carry with them their beliefs and understanding of the sacred. It should not be too surprising to find even in the most prosaic of neighborhoods, transplanted expressions of world religions and sects. Asian architectural design may reveal a Buddhist temple in the community. A Muslim tower on the urban horizon testifies to the growing global presence of the Islamic faith in the city.

New religious expressions, indeed, proliferate in the city. They are as controversial as the Church of Scientology and as provocative as New Age and spiritualist movements. Within the Hispanic landscape herbal medicinal shops sell religious artifacts. The "Botanica," as it is called, is sometimes affiliated with Santeria—one of those syncretistic religions that arrived from the Caribbean via Central America. Charismatic or Pentecostal groups are aggressively competing with Santeria, vying for the loyalty among immigrants from the Latin Hemisphere.

The Christian church now must compete for attention with a host of alternative pursuits, not to mention the forces creating the new urban world. The Christian story as articulated in the physical landscape now seems more and more to survive in random vestiges. Sometimes these remnants blend into the larger landscape and become hidden, lost or replaced.

These religious expressions in the built environment point to the irreducible fact of religious pluralism and other sources of cultural diversity that greatly increase the significance of the question about the locus of Christianity. In other words, given these global transfigurations what is the role of the Christian faith community in this new urban world? (Wulthnow, 1993)

In the postmodern conflicted and variegated landscape of the city, Christians must revisit who they are and what they are about. How are we to be defined? Do we stand for exclusivity and privilege or do we engender an attitude of acceptance and inclusion (not assimilation)? Do we foster class distinctions or reconciliation? Do we look toward ethnic affirmation and acculturation, or rote forms of ethnic cleansing and marginalization? Do we truly embody an ethic of service and caring? Do we bring a moral dimension to public life? Do we represent justice and mercy? Do we promote a deeper relationship to God? Do we reflect anything more than cultural ethnocentrism? Do we encourage economic and environmental responsibility? Are these values evident in the facilities that we build or renovate and the physical environment that we control?

The global dimensions of the contemporary urban world sets new challenges as new technologies and communications (i.e. social media) alter the way we live and relate. That the ministry and mission of the church must be realigned to take into account the global changes that are occurring is no longer an option. Andrew Davey, former resident urbanologist to the Council of Bishops for the Church of England, suggests that meeting the pastoral needs of ordinary people and struggling for social justice in our urban communities will inevitably take us into global territory (Davey, 2002). Addressing the concerns of an unemployed parishioner means considering the effects of the shifting global economy that forces the closure or relocation of factories and work. The financial quakes in Asia and Eastern Europe are quickly felt in both Madrid and Manhattan.

The polyethnic, multicultural realities of the urban landscape do indeed raise some profoundly unsettling questions not just as to the locus but the mission of the church. The Christian community can make a decisive contribution to this new era, however, in a manner different from the way it contributed during the past two millennia. A rethinking of the role of the church is critical if is to do so; an ecclesiology of cultural diversity is essential.

Global Village on the Urban Edge: Challenges for the Christian Church

The quest for community will be increasingly difficult in the coming years as technological and communication innovations foster new patterns of social engagement. Certainly, the rise of self-help groups reflects the need for community. So too do youth gangs and Internet chat rooms. Not discounting their benefits, sooner or later, people will discover that these groups or experiences do not suffice. At the same time, Christian-based communities or cell groups have already challenged the conventional concepts of "church."

The role of the Church may well go beyond community-building among believers. Admittedly, it may be tough going within a diverse and fluid urban culture, and yet in the long run more rewarding for the Christian Church to effect coalitions with neighborhood groups, civic associations, and nonprofit entities to work for broad objectives of economic, environmental, social and cultural justice. More important, the facilitating of community-building may prove to be a viable vehicle by which the message of the gospel can be clearly articulated and affirmed within the public arena.

But the church will be faced with much more than the task of bridging individuals, groups and organizations. Racial, ethnic, and regional divisions continue to be significant in the urban context, despite the facility of movement and contact. The widening chasm between the "haves" and "have nots," both politically and economically, will only magnify divisions corresponding to ethnic and geographic lines of separation.

One of the lessons learned from observing the emerging urban world is that the fault-lines of division are seldom static or easily discernible. For example, just when it appeared that boundaries between political and geographic rivals were beginning to erode, new tensions have appeared. Ideological battles are being waged on numerous fronts, challenging religious leaders to be responsibly involved in these conflicts as ministers of reconciliation. Moreover, attention must be given to the smaller or less vocal communities whose importance may be overshadowed by such tensions. Those of the dominant cultures have much to learn from those on the periphery.

Indeed, the main stimulus for rethinking the mission of the Church may well come from the bottom and from the edge, from those sectors of the world that have been on the fringes of the fading modern era. Places where Christians are poor, especially Africa and Latin America; from areas where Christian minorities are surrounded by non- Christian cultures, as in Asia; from the communities of faith that live under political oppression as they do in many parts of the world; from the churches of color and poor white; from those women who are agonizing together over what it means to be faithful and female in institutional structures that perpetuate patriarchy. These are the "voices from the margins," who have been forced to the sidelines, the basements, kitchens, slums, and colonies of the dominant culture. It is their struggle and hope that now enables them to offer a vision for the Church that may prove liberative because it has not been squeezed through some religious grid or distorted by the narrow function of mainstream religion.

Members of old-line denominations also have much to learn from younger denominations, independent movements and sects. In global terms the White minority has much to learn from the Ethnic majority. The fact of the matter is that we are embarking on a global path that challenges the notion of race and ethnicity as anthropological categories. Bi-racial and multi-ethnic families are no longer an anomaly but paradigm for human interaction. Contemporary social analysts are hard pressed as to what to call it. Jose Vasconcelos, some eighty years ago, gave us the term in his seminal work La Raza Cosmica (The Cosmic Race). (Vasconcelos, 1966 /1997). In the book he wrote about mestizaje (from "mestizo," meaning "mixed" or hybrid). This mestizaje or hybridity speaks of a "new people" originating from two or more ethnically disparate people. But the pioneers of the new multicultural urban world, as the global marketing forces have already discerned, may well be our global youth.

Our world cities have become incubators of a bold new mix of humanity. Our youth have created new social classifications for themselves: "white chocolate," "funky Aztecs" and "honorary homegirls." Such definitions wreak havoc with stubborn conventional stereotypes and archaic notions about what it is to be African, Asian or Caucasian in an ever-transfiguring urban world. Can we, the church, recognize God's image in one who is not in our image? Can we see "the new Eve," "the new Adam" among us?

While the institutional Church has much to learn from local indigenous and hybrid groups, still the message of Dr. Martin Luther King, Jr. reverberates in the urban village today: the beloved community must be lifted up. (King, Jr, 1957). Mere association does not make for community nor is a geographical collection of people a community. They shall know us by our love. The message is clear: we are to proclaim unity not uniformity, among our neighbors of the new urban village. In the spirit of reconciliation, a new sense of peoplehood is being called forth. The Church must be prepared to nurture the progenitors so that a healthy birth is experienced.

Clearly the challenges to the next Church require a sober assessment of the global future. But taking our Christian faith seriously argues strongly for an optimistic appraisal of the future. Perhaps Christianity's greatest contribution lies in the very orientation it poses toward the future itself. The Christian faith has always included a central message of hope; something learned from those who have struggled on the margins. As the world is being reshaped, that message will need to be clearly presented as never before.

As we have now entered the 21th century every aspect of what we call the urban context is indelibly marked by the powerful changes emanating from the globalization of our world and the advances within technology. The profound transformations in peoples, institutions, demography and geography are physically evident in the new urban reality. The continuous class and ethnic conflict, internal social disorder (communal, familial and individual), spiritual movements, and patterns of geographic mobility and economic stress have become part of our multicultural urban terrain where cities are crucibles of new civilizations in the making.

The Christian faith has never had a greater opportunity or a more urgent responsibility to live and proclaim its truths. The church faces challenges as it attempts to remain faithful to its roots and relevant to a polychromatic world. Yet its message of healing and hope, its ethic of hospitality and recognition of the face of Christ in that of the other, seems never to have been more needed. Christian response to these challenges demands discernment of the action of God in new ways, and this may mean ultimately carrying out faithful and bold ministry within postmodern forms yet to be conceived in the building of the New Jerusalem.

References

Castells, M. (1998). *The End of Millennium.* Hoboken, NJ: Blackwell.

Cox, H. (1984). *Religion in the Secular City: Toward a Postmodern Theology* NY, New York: Simon and Schuster.

Davey, A. P. (2002). *Urban Christianity and Global Order: Theological Resource for an Urban Future.* Peabody, MA: Hendrickson Publishers.

Schiller, G., Caglar, N. & Caglar, A. (2008). Migrant Incorporation and City Scale: Towards a Theory of Locality in Migration Studies. In *Willy Brandt Series of Working Papers in International Migration and Ethnic Relations,* Malmö University, Sweden.

Khanna, P. (2016) *Connectography: Mapping the Future of Global Civilization* NY, New York: Random House.

Kihato, W. K., Massooumi, M. & Ruble, B.A. (eds.). (2010). *Urban Diversity Space, Culture and Inclusive Pluralism in Cities Worldwide.* Washington DC, WA: Woodrow Wilson Center.

King, Jr., M. L. (1957). Advice for Living. (1957, November). *Ebony Magazine.*

Sandercock, L. (2013). *Cosmopolis II: Mongrel Cities of the 21st Century.* New York, NY: Bloomsbury.

Semuels, A. (2015, January 7). Suburbs and Areas and the New American Poverty. *The Atlantic.*

United Nations. (2014). *World Urbanization Prospects, 2014 Revision: Highlights.* Retrieved October, 2016 from http://esa.un.org/unpd/wup/Highlights/WUP2014-Highlights.pdf.

United Nations. (2016). *New Urban Agenda. Conference on Housing and Sustainable Urban Development (Habitat III),* Quito Ecuador.

Vasconcelos, J. (1966). La Raza Cosmíca: La Misión de la raza Iberoamericana. Aguilar. Ref. Jaen, D.T. (Trans.). (1997). *The Cosmic Race: A Bilingual Edition.* Baltimore, MD: John Hopkins University Press.

Wuthnow, R. (1993). *Christianity in the 21st Century: Reflections on the Challenges Ahead.* Oxford, England: Oxford University.

5

Shaping the World's Neighborhoods for Shalom

Chris Miller

Cities are acceleratingly the destinations of the world's population, and surely cities will be a primary focus of the Church. Knowing what we do about the ecological relation of inhabitants to the built environment, the Church can serve uniquely to shape neighborhoods and cities for shalom, the full flourishing of children, men and women in community.

Cities have become a significant focus of attention in the global north. Noah Toly (2016) notes a utopic confidence that the smart city is the sustainable technology. Also, there appears to be a political opposition between those who live in coastal global cities and the national hinterlands. For instance, in the UK's Brexit vote, London voted against Brexit as opposed to the rest of the country. Emily Badger, Quoctrung Bui, and Adam Pearce (2016) report that since the U.S. election there has been political opposition between city dwellers and others. The majority are under-represented and paying more taxes and live in the coastal cities.

In the exploding urban population of the 1840s, the British recognized their national responsibility through creating urban density and infrastructure for public well-being (Hebbert, 1999). The Americans have more recently connected public health to sprawling land development (Frumkin, Frank & Jackson, 2004). Concern in the relationship of public health to the built environment has been assessed recently:

There has been a shift in conceptualisations of health and disease from the treatment of illness in the individual to disease prevention and health promotion in populations. This has included increased focus on the impact of environments on collective well-being and on the interdependence of environments and individual behaviour (Kent & Thompson, 2012, p. 2).

This is consistent with the longstanding conclusion in longitudinal mortality studies that "... life expectancy in the modern world owes more to improved environmental hygiene than to the clinical interventions of doctors and hospitals (McKeown in Hebbert, 1999, p. 445).

Richard Sennett (2012), in the days after the 2015 Paris attacks, observed that failure to connect neighborhoods increases radicalization: he points to Christians gated in a Dresden neighborhood and to Muslims ostracized in Paris's suburbs and in Brussels's Molenbeek. Similarly, race mapping of American cities demonstrates remarkably that infrastructure (eg, an Interstate Highway, a rail line, or a high-volume street) creates social barriers and barriers to economic access (Badger & Cameron, 2015). Tragically, "... the unconnected city makes poor people poorer" (Cowan, 1997). Ursula Grant points out that it is necessary to "take geography seriously" (Grant, 2010, p.24).

Industrialized nations are re-discovering qualities of a highly-performing city but just as important, how it must appeal cognitively and even in beauty, to its inhabitants. Nan Ellin observes that, for the first time in the history of humankind, industrialized nations have developed unsustainable cities and that we are recovering what constitutes cities that are good for us (Ellin, 2013). Rising energy scarcity, climate change, and health are converging in demands for compact, vibrant cities: "well-planned, walkable communities have all of these characteristics

– adequate levels of density, a diversity of land uses, well-designed streetscapes and buildings, clear destinations for the pedestrian, and proximity to transit" (Ewing, et al. 2006). In middle-income and low-income urban poverty, the problem is not energy poverty but energy access (International Institute for Applied Systems Analysis, 2016). The qualities of the built environment are especially important to the support of the social ties forged in communities (Skjaeveland & Garling, 1997); it has been demonstrated that the built environment can constrain or promote passive contact amongst people (Talen, 2009). In urban design literature from 1985 to the present, there emerges a list of qualities constituting good places. Bentley, Alcock, Murrain, McGlynn, and Smith's (1985) *Responsive Environments: A Manual for Designers,* and most recently, Reid Ewing and Otto Clemente (2013) in *Measuring Urban Design: Metrics for Livable Places* demonstrate that these metric qualities can be used to evaluate the quality of urban environments: Imageability, enclosure, human scale, transparency, and complexity. These planning, urban design, and place-making principles seem to be a foundation of the New Urban Agenda which was adopted in October 2016 at Habitat III in Quito. It is expected that contributions from the cities of other cultures and societies will enable richer, more appropriate applications in particular places.

We will conclude with comments on the essential need for beauty in places. First, we will attend to the qualities that, in shaping a neighborhood, afford the formation of community for mutual benefit: permeability, variety, legibility, robustness, human scale and enclosure, and patterns.

Permeability

The most enjoyable cities are the ones that present the fewest barriers between people, uses, activities, and places (Cowan, 1997). A recent investigation of permeability concludes that "… the most walkable grids are those that maximize the number of [building lots] one can reach within a given walking radius while minimizing the travel distance required to reach them" (Hansen, 1959, p. 91). City block dimensions and building lot width matter: the rectangular Manhattan block, accommodating many narrow lots, and the small square Portland block present the greatest number of destinations to pedestrians in a 1000m pedestrian shed. Theoretically, the Manhattan block with its 8m wide lots could present more destinations by shortening the length of the block to 168m and lots to 21; the Portland block, with 15m lot widths, could be improved by increasing the number of lots from 4 to 10. Row houses, in West London just 15m (16.5ft) wide with blocks similar to those of Manhattan, are modeled to yield 10,000 destinations (Rasmussen, 1934). Portland's blocks are not too different from those prescribed in the British New Town Act of 1662 for colonial American towns (Reps, 1965). "All else being equal, in improving pedestrian accessibility, reducing plot frontages is the most effective adjustment ..." (Sevtsuk, Kalvo & Ekmekci, 2016, p. 99). In what can be called fine-grained urbanism, shorter, shallower block shapes and narrow lot widths are scaled to our capacities for visual stimulation and walking.

For example, in the photograph above of London's Woburn Walk, see that the doors to the flats above and the shop doors demonstrate the fine-grain urbanism with an interval of about 20 feet.

Jane Jacobs concludes from empirical observation that the permeability of small blocks affords affiliation and mutuality. A corner café can be undertaken more easily by neighbors in smaller, equal blocks and streets than a tree-like block-and-street system that concentrates traffic and elevates land values (Jacobs, 1961). A local venture can be supported in mutuality with the profits and social benefits staying local (American Independent Business Alliance).

The character of a town arises from its long-standing street and block arrangement, from its slow-changing fabric of building and place types, and least from its most flexible land uses (Conzen, 1981). The character of a place, in its permeable urbanism and its building types, is physical with a particular rootedness from which can arise the local identity of persons and communities.

Justness can be realized in the accessibility by all to plazas and streets as a political right; there must be a place for public speech. As cities are privatized, we seek increasingly the peace of not being addressed for commercial purposes. In *The World Outside Your Head*, Matthew B. Crawford observes that increasingly the elite find for themselves sanctuaries from being addressed as the public realm is dominated by commercial interests. In *Sidewalks in the Kingdom,* it is observed that the Church may be an agent in preserving places in which we can address each other politically (Jacobsen, 2003).

It may be that the Church is not coming late to its concern for the ecological built environment. The first modern treatise on architecture, written by L.B. Alberti, a priest who offered his work to God's glory, adopts the notion that we share the capacity to judge the beauty of civic urbanism and that all, inhabitants and strangers alike, should have access to the agricultural hinterland, to the market, to hospice care, to the city's protection, and to its streets generally (Miller, in draft). Eric Jacobsen reflects that cities of Western urbanism, so many founded and sometimes with real intention, as Christian cities can be probed as efforts to build by a system of Christian values but also those by whom all would flourish. Understanding more clearly than ever the contribution of the built environment to our emotional and physical health, the beautiful place is permeable, by citizens and strangers, to food, protection, care, employment, light, air, and parks.

Compact Variety

The value of design promotes diversity and choice through a mix of compatible developments and uses that work together to create viable places that respond to local needs (Commission for Architecture and the Built Environment and Department of the Environment, Transport and the Regions, 2001). Diversity itself has been found a good thing in a number of fields: mixtures of, rather than separated uses (Jacobs, 1961), social and economic exchange possibilities (Greenberg, 1995 and Mumford, 1938); and a mixture of housing, schools, and shopping (Hayden, 2003). Jane Jacobs (1961) writes that a sustainable urbanism possesses lively, populous diversity built on four principles: multi-use blocks, blocks of particular sizes, "'close-grained' mingling" of mostly older and some newer buildings, and lots of people who live and work there (Jacob, 1961, p. 141).

First, compact variety must support a dense and diverse residential population. There are living arrangements that are a choice across the entire spectrum from the wealthiest to the least not just those who have particular levels of income (Rasmussen, 1934). A plurality of housing types, arising from a mix of building lot and block sizes, can accommodate a variety of economic strata (Jacobs, 1961). This fine-grained urbanism increases the potential in narrow lots giving rise to proportionally scaled buildings so that there is yet family resemblance in the range of residential and commercial types; in turn, this sets off the civic institutions as being those that are collectively held important. Variety is misused to represent the differences between the owners of the same or similar commercial uses. Density can yield a diversity with critical mass to support the cultural interests of the majority and the minorities (Jacobs, 1961).

Variety in shopping can keep what the poor need within their means of acquisition. The aim in variety is to draw varied people including those with low modality, in varying numbers, at varied times producing a range of activities being interpreted in a variety of ways (Bentley, et al., 1985).

Second, a vibrant urbanism requires a great number of distinct and different land uses in the fine-grain of smaller blocks with many and narrow-fronted lots. Jane Jacobs recognized the need for a variety of businesses to keep the streets busy with, and therefore safe for, pedestrians. The quality of variety aims to intensify for safety and effectiveness the activity of streets by the mixing of pedestrian and vehicular movement on streets. The land uses can be chosen and positioned strategically to foster sidewalk activity in evening and night hours (Jacobs, 1961).

Third, are older buildings inter-mingled with some newer buildings. Varying ages of buildings are essential for incubating and long-lived institutions, like churches who provide the diachronic component to the social ecosystem. Jacobs writes that public uses and buildings should stand "staunchly" (Jacob, 1961, p. 254). Jacobs again states that new buildings can be mingled among a majority of older buildings arguing that small businesses survive in the low-cost situation they find in old buildings while only the highly profitable or highly subsidized businesses or not for profits can afford the costs of demolition and new building (Jacobs, 1961).

Fine-grained urbanism comprises buildings with floor widths no greater than twice their floor-to-ceiling heights, because these are shaped to passive systems, consume modest amounts of energy in comparison to energy-consuming, active systems for heating, cooling, and ventilating (Ratti, Baker & Steemers, 2005). More so than the long buildings set in open land, courtyard houses have been demonstrated to be efficient in land use and in accessing light (Broadbent, 1990). In regards to transportation, energy use and carbon dioxide production, cities with the density, building height, and compactness of Stockholm are highly efficient (Worldwatch Institute).

Compact density provides the ridership that makes transit an affordable, civic amenity. Sprawl, without this density, privileges those with individual transit and the under-resourced and limited transit system is used only by the poor. Jacobs writes: "... automobiles are hardly inherent destroyers of cities" (Jacobs, 1961, p. 343). It is, rather, the traffic that has a hugely negative impact on cities in numerous ways: "The mechanical vehicles, in their overabundance, work slothfully and idle much" (Jacobs, 1961, p. 343). It is the space required for this overabundance of automobiles in movement and in storage that forces a dissolution of cities that in the suburbs is described as sprawl (Jacobs, 1961).

Jane Jacobs observes there is also that population diversity that cannot be attributed to perceived economic benefit but who reside in places out of transcendent motivations, perhaps cohering round an institution, for which a planner cannot account or plan (Jacobs, 1961). Similar is Chesterton's observation that people love places and in loving them, make them beautiful (Chesterton, 1908). This affection for locality in place can rise from several sources that includes those spiritual pioneers who move to a neighborhood, out of the love of God, to love their neighbors there.

Legibility

A foundational study on how we read meaning into places determined an interplay of three perceptions. Legibility of a city depends on congruence of significance, activity, and type: does the city's permeability feature for our experience the most important activities in appropriate building and place types (Steinitz, 1967)? A city, whose inhabitants want its meaning to read transparently, will arrange its blocks, streets, and lots, together with its land-use variety so that the most highly communicative buildings are set apart for our perception and are the settings for our most important activities. If these are active aspirations for worship, for peace, for justice, citizens may have places that both declare and teach their hopes and values.

Formal categories for legibility include nodes, edges, paths, districts, and landmarks (Bentley et al.; Lynch & Steinitz). Nodes are those places that feature an activity. An edge presents a fundamental and describable difference of use or in pair of uses from one side to the other marking the borders of one district to another. Path describes the streets, afforded by a place's permeability the following of which are either navigated by or seek a landmark. Landmarks are those places whose embodied congruence can be read by people on the street as legibly significant.

Imageability is the quality of a place that makes it distinct, recognizable, and memorable. A place has high imageability when specific physical elements and their arrangement capture attention, evoke feelings, and create a lasting impression (Ewing et. al, 2006).

Above, in the photograph of Quito's basilica, the colonial quarter demonstrates the legibility in a permeable block arrangement that opens to the hilltop situation of the basilica; the activity that we can witness there is consistent with the representation in the architecture. Historic Quito manifests a legibility in which its important institutions can be read reliably.

Robustness

Robust buildings and places are those that are abundant in their affordances: they lend themselves to many purposes, both simultaneously and successively. Places can be made robust for multiple uses and throughout a day when a desirable microclimate is shaped (Bentley et al 1985). Brittle, on the other hand, are those buildings and places shaped so slavishly to a particular use that they are abandoned and replaced when uses change (Sennett, 2015). Robustness supports vitality time and again because the buildings, like the townhouses or the courtyard house and places afford re-purposing in one generation after another. Regarding the robustness of architectural types, see the analysis of Peter Cowan in Broadbent (1973).

Human Scale and Enclosure

Richness or complexity increases the choice and breadth of sensate experiences including the aural and tangible (Bentley et al, 1985 & Ewing et al, 2006). Human scale "refers to a size, texture, and articulation of physical elements that match the size and proportions of humans and equally important, correspond to the speed at which humans walk.. Building details, pavement texture, street trees, and street furniture are all physical elements contributing to human scale" (Ewing et al, 2006 p. 226). Scaled too, are city blocks; preindustrial cities had blocks of no longer than 1,200 feet (Porta & Romice, 2010, p. 16). Studies continue to confirm the pedestrian shed, quarter-mile or two furlong radius (1320ft) Some have found that pre-industrial cities, still those that are most enjoyable, are characterized by plazas or similar at every furlong (Duany 2014).

Enclosure describes places having a desirable room-like proportion (Ewing & Clemente, 2013). Comfortable plazas are rarely longer than twice their width and if longer than 137m, then beyond human scale (Alberti, 1965). Enclosure requires building heights no less than half the width of the narrow dimension of a plaza; best is a 1 to 1 ratio of building height to the plaza's narrow dimension (Sitte, 1889).

A street neighborhood is a social ecosystem in which the many exercise "a modicum of public responsibility" securing tolerance and safety for everyone including children, the infirm, and strangers (Jacobs, 1961) and private interactions (Bentley et al, 1985). What makes a street that affords this civic virtue?

The border of public place to private place is an ecosystem interface of physical and visual permeability. First, each building presents its public façade to the street and with its neighboring buildings creates a street wall that encloses the street and separates the public street from the block interior comprised of private backs of buildings, private yards, and semi-public alleys (Bentley et al., 1985). Places, streets, alleys, and yards foster a positive, high degree of territoriality when each is clearly circumscribed and owner or stewardship is uncontested (van Nes & Lopez, 2007).

Second, public responsibility is afforded by constituted places and streets. A street is constituted when at least 75% of the framing buildings have shallow, direct access to the street. Most secure are buildings on streets with at least 75% inter-visibility: inter-visible buildings have entrances and windows that are visible from the entrances and windows of buildings facing from across the street (van Nes & Lopez, 2007). Society and cultural habits may determine the density of entrances.

In the photograph above of Stockholm's medieval quarter, the pacing of doors and windows exemplifies a constituted street with a high degree of inter-visibility from the street's residences and shops. These streets are examples of the human scale and enclosure including active and attractive streets and are consistent with the metrics that have been advanced to quantify what meets our human capacities.

Building type brings the quality of enclosure to securing a street in mutuality. Flats, with lines of sight longer than 15m to and from the street, may be too far removed to influence the safety of the street below (Sussman & Hollander, 2015). North Hanover Street, in Boston's Beacon Hill, is an example with a street width of approximately 16m (3 rods) and flanking three-story flats of residential types. Least effective for effecting mutual security on a street would be residential types with flats higher than three stories above the street or with corridors with long connections to a central stair or with doors that do not engage the street directly.

Patterns

From the current state of brain science and how we respond to places and buildings, there are a number of conclusions: for example, "Patterns Matter" (Sussman & Hollander, 2015). Recognizing that our minds query the meaning of the environment, the symbolism of buildings and places figure in the making and keeping of good cities. In this light, visual appropriateness is the legible symbolism in the representation of a particular institution, whether a church or family; and, it can be the appropriateness of a particular institution relative to other particular institutions (Bentley et al, 1985).

> Visual appropriateness is particularly important in the places which are most likely to be frequented by people from a wide variety of different backgrounds; particularly when the place's appearance cannot be altered by the users themselves. Both indoors and out, therefore, visual appropriateness is mostly important in the more public spaces of the scheme. So far as public outdoor space is

concerned, it is particularly relevant to the outside of the buildings which define the public realm (Bently et al., 1985, p. 76).

In the image above, from Venice's Burano, there is a clear pattern of residential building types. Even with the variety of two and three-bay wide houses and the mix of two and three story buildings, there is the chimney front and the chimney side types. This single difference suggests a house plan that distinguishes one from the other. These are patterns, that we perceive, and on reflection, understand cognitively. Our intention to find meaning in the environment yields such and reinforces our interest.

We ask whether the symbolic content that we read is congruent with the apparent use of the place of building. We deduce a use from the appearance and expect that the building's cues have expressed that use; we are confused when our attempt to interpret meaning is frustrated. A philosopher reasons that "[w]e cannot just judge that something is beautiful; we just judge that it is beautiful in virtue of its [symbolic content]" (Zangwill, 2010). We want to know what the building is before we make a judgment about its beauty; that is, we want to judge first whether the reading of the building's symbolic content is appropriate to the building's identity. We might say that, yes, the building looks like a church; now I can decide whether this appropriate representation is beautiful or not.

Theology and Beauty

Nicholas Wolterstorff's observations on urban life in *Art and Action* capture two of the major challenges facing those who reside in and plan for cities; so much of what we see in cities fails to delight, and so many of our cities' inhabitants are marginalized and disempowered (Wolterstorff, 1980). *Sidewalks in the Kingdom* argues that the markers of a good city may be argued theologically. A good city is a kind of common grace and is perhaps our practice for the New Jerusalem. A good city has places that can and are shared by all its inhabitants. Based on the value and dignity of all ethnic communities and to all persons, whether citizens of or strangers to a place, we should see our cities as places extending hospitality and not merely food, protection, and care.

Good cities are safe places for those perhaps not empowered politically to have a voice; also, the political space for the Church and its people to speak to culture, to power, and particularly for peace and for justness.

There is a settled confidence that thriving places are those built environments tuned to human scale over many generations in which incremental adjustments and additions, rather than colossal experiments, are undertaken. There has been a return to the observations that can be learned from a particular place and applied, in scale, to another place. Scruton (2014) points to a myriad of aesthetic adjustments by which a community adapts their built environment to their collective sense of the appropriate. Wolterstorff (1980) might say that a city, from whom its endowment of beauty figures importantly, builds forward in hope of wholeness for individuals and collectively. Living together and well, Scruton (2009) writes, is an end of interest in beauty: ... argument does not aim to win by whatever means, but rather to generate a consensus... Implicit in our sense of beauty is the thought of community – of the agreement in judgments that makes social life possible and worthwhile.

This appears to be attested in two recent surveys. In 2010, the British Commission for Architecture and the Built Environment published

People and Places: Public Attitudes To Beauty. The British government, seeing the political and social need to be more deliberately inclusive, surveyed public attitudes toward beauty in hopes that this would be an area in which a common social consciousness could be cultivated (Ipsos MORI, 2010). In excerpts the report states:

> Not only are people ready to hear and to engage in a national debate on the subject, they call for beauty to be reinstated as a public value with meaning that stretches beyond the latest trends in fashion, hair, even architecture (Ipsos MORI, 2010, p. 3).

And:

> Perhaps one of the most striking areas of consensus was in the value people placed on old... buildings... Across all age groups, older buildings were invariably favoured as being more beautiful (Ipsos MORI, 2010, p. 35).

Secondly, in the "Ten Principles for Building Healthy Places" that points to the results of the "Soul of the Community" study:

> In 2010, the Knight Foundation partnered with the Gallup organization to survey 43,000 residents of 26 U.S. cities to determine what attracts people to a place and keeps them there. The study found that the most important factors that create emotional bonds between people and their communities were not jobs, but rather "physical beauty, opportunities for socializing, and a city's openness to all people." The Knight Foundation also found that communities with the highest levels of attachment to place also had the strongest economies. Cohesive communities also report higher levels of safety and security, community activity, and emotional health and well-being. Community involvement and political participation are associated with improved health outcomes; for instance, one study found a direct link between group membership and reduced mortality rates (Knight Foundation, 2013, p. 24).

We begin to understand, from a Christian perspective, the anthropologica and social implications in a particular built ecosystem and its potentia of nudging men, women, and children toward flourishing. We can make justness in places, a kind of beauty or shalom for our families and for ou neighbors.

References

Alberti, L.B. (1435). On Painting in Vitruvius, *Ten books on architecture.* NY New York: Random House.

Sitte, C. (1889). City Planning According to Artistic Principles in Vitruvius, *Ter books on architecture.* NY, New York: Random House.

The Multiplier Effect of Local Independent Businesses. (2016). Retrieved fror http://www.amiba.net/resources/multiplier-effect#ixzz2nwAqyx73.

Badger, E., Bui, Q., & Pearce, A. (2016). The election highlighted a growin rural-urban split. *New York Times.* Retrieved from http://www.nytimes com/2016/11/12/upshot/this-election-highlighted-a-growing-rural-urban- split.html.

Badger, E. & Cameron, D. (2015). How railroads, highways, and other man- made lines racially divide America's cities. *Washington Post.* Retrieved fror https://www.washingtonpost.com/news/wonk/wp/2015/07/16/how-railroads- highways-and-other-man-made-lines-racially-divide-americas-cities/.

Bentley, I., Alcock, A., Murrain, P., McGlynn, S., & Smith, G. (1985). *Responsive environments: A manual for designers.* London, England: Architectural Press.

Broadbent, G. (1990). *Emerging concepts in urban space design.* London England: E & FN Spon.

Chesterton, G.K. (1908). *Orthodoxy.* United Kingdom: Hendrickson.

Commission for Architecture and the Built Environment and Departmen of the Environment, Transport and the Regions. (2001). *Urban Design.* Kent, England: Thomas Telford.

Conzen, M.R. (1981). *The urban landscape: Historical development and management: Papers by M.R.G. Conzen.* London, England: Academic Press.

Cowan, R. (1997). *The Connected City: A New Approach to Making Cities Work.* Melbourne, Australia: Urban Initiatives.

Cowan, R. (1973). Studies in the growth, change, and ageing of buildings. *Design in Architecture: Architecture and the Human Sciences.* Broadbent, G. (Ed.). Somerset, NJ: Wiley.

Crawford, M.B. (2015). *The World Outside Your Head: How to flourish in an age of distraction.* New York, NY: Farrar, Straus and Giroux.

Duany, D. (2014). Orvieto, Italy. V. Dover & J. Massengale. (Eds.). *Street design: The secret of great cities and towns.* New Jersey, NY: John Wiley & Sons.

Ellin, N. (2013). *Good urbanism: Six steps to creating prosperous places.* Washington DC, WA: Island Press.

Ewing, R., Handy, S., Brownson, R., Clemente, O. & Winston, E. (2006). Identifying and measuring urban design qualities related to walkability. *Journal of Physical Activity and Health, 3(1),* S223-S240. in Chicago Metropolitan Agency for Planning / Urban Design / Definition. Retrieved from http://www.cmap.illinois.gov/about/2040/supporting-materials/process-archive/strategy-papers/urban-design/definition.

Ewing, R. & Clemente, O. (2013). *Measuring for urban design: Metrics for liveable places.* Washington DC, WA: Island Press.

Frumkin, H., Frank, L., & Jackson, R. (2004). *Urban sprawl and public health.* Washington DC, WA: Island Press.

Grant, U. (2010). *Spatial Inequality and Urban Poverty Traps.* London, England: Overseas Development Institute Chronic Poverty Research Centre.

Hebbert, M. (1999). A city in good shape: Town planning and public health. *The Town Planning Review. 70(4),* 433-453.

International Institute for Applied Systems Analysis. (2016). Energy access and housing for the urban poor. *Urban Energy Systems.* Retrieved from http://www.iiasa.ac.at/web/home/research/Flagship-Projects/Global-Energy-Assessment/GEA_Chapter18_urban_lowres.pdf.

Ipsos MORI. (2010). Public attitudes to beauty. United Kingdom: *Commission for Architecture and the Built Environment.*

Jacobs, J. (1961). *The death and life of great American cities.* New York, NY: Random House.

Jacobsen, E. (2003). *Sidewalks in the kingdom.* Grand Rapids, MI: Brazos.

Kent, J. & Thompson, S. (2012). Health and the built environment: Exploring foundations for a new interdisciplinary profession. *Journal of Environmental and Public Health,* 2012, (2).

McMahon, E.T., Eitler, T. & Thoerig, T.C. (2013). *The ten principles for building healthy places.* Washington DC, WA: Urban Land Institute.

Miller, C. (in draft). Bella Citta.

Newman & J.R. Kenworth. (2007). Urban density and transport-related energy consumption. In P. Bovet, P. Rekacewicz, A. Sinai & D. Vidal (eds.). *Atlas Environement du Monde Diplomatique.*

Porta, S. & Romice, O. (2010). *Plot-based urbanism: Towards time-consciousness in place-making.* Glasgow, Scotland: Urban Design Studies Unit, University of Strathclyde, Department of Agriculture.

Rasmussen, S. E. (1934). *London: The unique city.* Cambridge, MA: MIT Press.

Ratti, C. Baker, N., & Steemers, K. (2005). Energy consumption and urban texture. *Energy and Buildings, 37(7),* 762-776.

Reps, J.W. (1965). *The making of urban America: A history of city planning in the United States.* Princeton, NJ: Princeton University Press.

Scruton, R. (2014). Lecture. *Order and fluidity: Reflections on post-modern architecture.* Notre Dame University School of Architecture.

Scruton, R. (2009). *Beauty.* Oxford, England: Oxford University Press.

Sennett, R. (2015). The Open City. Retrieved from http://www.richardsennett.com/site/senn/templates/general2.aspx?pageid=38&cc =gb.

Sevtsuk, A., Kalvo, R., & Ekmekci, O. (2016). Pedestrian accessibility in grid layouts: The role of block, plot, and street dimensions. *Urban Morphology, 20(2)*, 91-99.

Sitte, C. (1889). *City Planning According to Artistic Principles.* Translated English Edition (1965): New York, NY: Random House Press.

Steinitz, C.F. *Congruence and meaning: The influence of consistency between urban form and activity upon environmental knowledge.* PhD Dissertation: MIT.

Sterret, R. (2015, November 27). The world wants more 'porous' cities – so why don't we build them? *Guardian.* Retrieved from https://www.theguardian.com/cities/2015/nov/27/delhi-electronic-market-urbanist-dream.

Sussman, A. & Hollander, J.B. (2015). *Cognitive architecture: Designing for how we respond to the built environment.* New York, NY: Rutledge.

Talen. E., (2009). *Urban Design Reclaimed: Tools, Techniques and strategies for planners.* Victoria, Canada: AbeBooks.

Toly, N. (2016, September 15). Century of the city: The Promises & Limitations of 21st Century Urbanism: Practices making community. *James Didier Symposium on Christ & Architecture.* Judson University.

UN Habitat. (2016). *New Urban Agenda.* Retrieved from https://habitat3.org/the-new-urban-agenda/.

Van Nes, A. & Lopez, M.J. (2007). Micro scale spatial relationships in urban studies: The relationship between private and public space and its impact on street life. *Proceedings, 6th International Space Syntax Symposium, Istanbul.*

Wolterstorff, N. (1980). *Art in action: Towards a Christian aesthetic.* Grand Rapids, MI: Eerdmans.

Worldwatch Institute. *An international sourcebook of automobile dependence in cities, 1960-1990.* Boulder, CO: University Press of Colorado.

Zangwill, N. (2010). Aesthetic judgment. *The Stanford Encyclopedia of Philosophy.* Zalta, E.N. (Ed.). Retrieved from http://plato.stanford.edu/archives/fall2010/entries/aesthetic-judgment/

Section 2

Applying Shalom

Transforming the Lives of Urban Children & Youth Through Asset Building

6

Bryan McCabe

For the past eleven years I have had the opportunity to participate in leading a youth mentoring initiative in a marginalized urban neighborhood in Pittsburgh, Pennsylvania. Our local church has facilitated more than 400 mentoring matches with urban children and youth during that time, and more than a dozen other churches in the city have also provided mentors to vulnerable kids in our city. God has given me a strong calling to participate in his redemptive mission with the young people and families in my city. I moved my family right next door to the local elementary school where most of the children in the mentoring program attend, so I have had an up close and personal view of the amazing process of transformation that has taken place in the lives of both the young people being mentored and the adult volunteers who are serving as mentors. God is working through the mentoring relationships to transform lives and transform the neighborhood.

There has been a steady stream of humanity coming through our home since we moved into the neighborhood. Our dinner table has been visited by all kinds of different people. My two daughters have become friends with a lot of the kids in the neighborhood who are especially drawn to our house because of our trampoline in the back yard, the homework help that we're sometimes able to offer, and lots of fun that our family has with games, block parties, popsicles, street chalk on our sidewalk, and our ukulele jam sessions. We have a lot of fun. Recently, one of the kids who comes over to our house all the time, Keyshawn, stopped over for a visit with a big grin and a piece of paper in his hands. He handed the piece of paper over to my wife, Julie, and me and he said, "Check out my school assignment. I was asked to write a poem about Pittsburgh." He had moved to Pittsburgh a few years ago after spending most of his childhood in Boston, so I wasn't sure what to expect. What kind of poem would he write? In the part of Pittsburgh where we live, there is often a lot of negative press and perceptions about violence and crime. Would he write about the negative things in his neighborhood?

I was pleasantly surprised by what he chose to write about his city. Here's what he wrote:

Newfound Home

By
Keyshawn

I've heard some inspiring
things about Pittsburgh
I've even seen
some things too.
People here rep their
hoods with pride.
Little league football
teams excel.
Neighbors help each
other.
Bridges everywhere,
along with buses
always packed.

But young boys and girls
never stray from giving
up their seat for the
elderly.
So even though I miss
Boston,
seeing the fireworks
going off on the 4th of July
downtown,
seeing the water
glistening
on all 3 rivers makes all
the difference.
Downtown is a food hub
from Italian food, Chinese
food, and Greek food all
on the same block.
I now understand why
people say Pittsburgh is
one of the best cities in
the world!

Instead of choosing to describe brokenness, he chose to write about the assets in his city. He covered a lot of ground in a relatively small amount of words. The assets he wrote about include neighbors, youth sports leagues, bridges (supposedly Pittsburgh is the city with the second highest amount of bridges in the world behind only Vienna, Italy), public transportation, compassionate kids, older adults, fireworks, a downtown economic center with a beautiful skyline, rivers, excellent and diverse cuisine, and appreciative residents. He didn't just describe landmarks, though. He managed to capture the heart and soul of Pittsburgh, a city that he now sees as his home. These are challenging words from an urban youth. Do I love my city as much as Keyshawn loves his city? Does my church love this city as much as he does?

In a conversation a few days later, I asked Keyshawn if he could list some more assets about his neighborhood. While he was eating something like his fifth packet of fruit snacks at my kitchen table (my grocery bill has gone up considerably since he started spending so much time at our house), he said, "Lots of sports stars, the YMCA, the library, basketball and football pick up games, smart people, a community swimming pool, community gardens, schools, shops, a bakery, bus stops and lots of buses, and a fire station."

I asked him if he could list some assets that he has. He said, "Well, I'm funny, smart, and athletic. I have good hair. I have a dad, a house with my own room, a good church with a youth leader that I like, a good school, solid teachers, great friends, and, of course, my pit bulls." I don't know about the pit bulls. They always bark at me when I walk past his house, but I guess they qualify as assets since they provide such intimidating protection.

I'm sharing Keyshawn's perspective on his city because, although he is just one of billions of urban children and youth in our world, his voice matters. Young people have so much to contribute to our world, and urban youth empowerment is an excellent way to facilitate transformation in cities.

The New Urban Agenda and Sustainable Development Goals

The challenges facing urban children and youth was a significant focus of the UN's Habitat III. In the New Urban Agenda ratified in Quito, October 2016, stakeholders committed to "promote access for youth to education, skills development and employment to achieve increased productivity and shared prosperity in cities and human settlements. Girls and boys, young women and young men, are key agents of change in creating a better future and when empowered, they have great potential to advocate on behalf of themselves and their communities. Ensuring more and better opportunities for their meaningful participation will be essential for the implementation of the New Urban Agenda" (UN Habitat, 2016, p.9).

Children and youth are specifically highlighted as a people group of emphasis throughout the New Urban Agenda document, including in paragraphs 20, 34, 39, 42, 48, 57, 61, 148, and 155. Urban children and youth are also deeply impacted by many of the other areas of focus such as, housing, violence, food security, diseases, and climate change. The New Urban Agenda presents an opportunity for meaningful transformation in cities throughout the world. "This New Urban Agenda reaffirms our global commitment to sustainable urban development as a critical step for realizing sustainable development in an integrated and coordinated manner at global, regional, national, sub-national, and local levels, with the participation of all relevant actors. The implementation of the New Urban Agenda contributes to the implementation and localization of the 2030 Agenda for Sustainable Development in an integrated manner, and to the achievement of the Sustainable Development Goals (SDGs) and targets, including SDG 11 of making cities and human settlements inclusive, safe, resilient, and sustainable" (UN Habitat, 2016, p.1).

In addition to SDG 11, focusing on urban children and youth may also have a direct impact on the following Sustainable Development Goals:

- Goal 1. End poverty in all its forms everywhere
- Goal 3. Ensure healthy lives and promote well-being for all at all ages
- Goal 4. Ensure inclusive and equitable quality education and promote lifelong learning opportunities for all
- Goal 5. Achieve gender equality and empower all women and girls
- Goal 10. Reduce inequality within and among countries
- Goal 16. Promote peaceful and inclusive societies for sustainable development, provide access to justice for all, and build effective, accountable and inclusive systems at all levels (UN General Assembly, 2015, p.14).

Signs of Need in Urban Children and Youth

Rapid global urbanization has caused many young people living in cities to become increasingly vulnerable. According to UNICEF, "153 million kids worldwide have lost one or both parents due to all causes" (Childinfo). Millions of children reside in urban slum and squatter neighborhoods.

Urban children growing up in poverty is a global issue, and it is also a national issue where I live in the United States. "In the United States, 21 percent of all children are in poverty. This poverty rate is higher than what prevails in virtually all other rich nations" (Stanford Centre on Poverty and Inequality). In the United States of America National Report for the Third United Nations Conference on Housing and Sustainable Urban Development (Habitat III), the authors of the report chose to highlight the plight of urban children and youth. "While life for urban youth continues to improve throughout the United States, not all urban youth have the same experiences. Poverty, crime, and school dropout rates disproportionately affect African-American youth and other minorities" (US Dept of Housing and Urban Development). The poverty rate is also high for minority populations in America. "In 2013, the poverty rate was 36.9 percent for African-American children, compared to 30.4 percent for Hispanic children and 10.7 percent for non-Hispanic White children" (Office Assistant Secretary for Planning and Evaluation, 2014). The authors of the U.S. report to Habitat III also listed education and homelessness as significant issues impacting urban children and youth.

There are many signs of need related to urban children and youth globally such as poverty, violence, neglect, homelessness, drug and alcohol abuse, gangs, racism, classism, suicide, HIV/AIDS, and human trafficking. The list could go on and on with issues like, mass incarceration, unemployment, and fatherlessness that have a deep impact on how young people are developing in our world.

Author and activist Cornel West describes how all of these factors can lead to a sense of hopelessness and despair for vulnerable urban children and youth. "The collapse of meaning in life – the eclipse of hope and absence of love of self and others, the breakdown of family and neighborhood bonds – leads to the social deracination and cultural denudement of urban dwellers, especially children. We have created rootless, dangling people with little link to the supportive networks – family, friends, school – that sustain some sense of purpose in life… The result is lives of what we might call 'random nows,' of fortuitous and fleeting moments preoccupied with 'getting over' – with acquiring pleasure, property, and power by any means necessary" (West, 1993, p.10).

Even though children and youth face many challenges, development responses that focus too much on deficits can actually cause more harm than good. Punitive responses involving negative labeling of young people often lead to ineffective outcomes such as mass incarceration or shortsighted relief attempts that further expand cycles of poverty. "Service organizations by defining youth exclusively in terms of their problems and needs help to create barriers that make it difficult for young people to become productive members of the community. Thus youth can easily become trapped in a cycle of ongoing dependency, and the community itself will lose some of its greatest potential assets. Given the proper opportunities, however, youth can always make a significant contribution to the development of the communities in which they live. What is needed for this to happen are specific projects that will connect youth with the community in ways that will increase their own self-esteem and level of competency while at the same time improving the quality of life of the community as a whole" (Kretzmann & McKnight, 1993, p.29).

Signs of Hope in Urban Children and Youth

Development work with children and youth should focus on asset building through relationship-based approaches leading to a process of transformation. Urban youth can demonstrate remarkable courage, resilience, faith, compassion, passion, intelligence, and humor while navigating through the challenges that the city presents. Children have many assets that can be developed in order to contribute to society, including "time, ideas and creativity, connection to place, dreams and desires, peer group relationships, family relationships, credibility as teachers, enthusiasm and energy" (Kretzmann & McKnight, 1993, p.30-31).

Urban children and youth have hope. "Hope is a strange thing. It dreams of and believes in what is not seen. Hope always sits in a place between what is real and what is longed for. Once something you've hoped for becomes reality, hope is no longer necessary. Hope, like faith, always invests in what is unseen and what is most unimaginable" (Ruthruff, 2010, p.168).

The Search Institute has identified forty "building blocks of healthy development – known as Developmental Assets – that help young people grow up healthy, caring, and responsible. Twenty external assets fall into the categories of support, empowerment, boundaries and expectations, and constructive use of time, while twenty internal assets fall into the categories of commitment to learning, positive values, social competencies, and positive identity" (Search Institute). This organization has generated tremendous research that has helped to support asset-based approaches to transforming the lives of urban children and youth in the United States and around the world.

As with all human beings made in the image of God, urban children and youth have many signs of hope. Desmond Tutu, a Christian leader who has an amazing ability to look for the best in people despite challenging circumstances, points out that, "Each of us has a capacity for great good and that is what makes God say it was well worth the risk to bring us into existence. Extraordinarily, God the omnipotent One depends on us, puny, fragile, vulnerable as we may be, to accomplish God's purposes for good, for justice, for forgiveness and healing and wholeness. God has no one but us" (Tutu, 1999, p.158).

Cities Have Many Assets

Cities have many assets. It is important to connect the assets that urban children and youth have to the assets in the city in order to bring about individual and community transformation. If isolation is one of the biggest factors related to poverty, then connecting young urban people to the people engaged in the systems throughout a city assists with overcoming isolation through healthy, meaningful relationships. Thinking about how to engage urban children and youth in city transformation can seem like an overwhelming task because our modern cities can be overwhelmingly complex. Thankfully, we have many great resources that urban ministry practitioners and academics have developed to assist with the process.

In *To Transform a City*, Eric Swanson and Sam Williams present a wonderful overview of some ways that Christians are beginning to approach cities from asset-based approaches instead of deficit-based approaches. The authors suggest that, "Cities, especially large ones, often seem like these impenetrable, amorphous entities that resist any and all efforts at transformation" (Swanson & Williams, 2010, p.147). The process of transformation can occur in cities, though, and Christians can lead the way. "Each city, regardless of geography or ethnography, can be divided into these three sectors – the private sector, the public sector, and the social sector" (Swanson & Williams, 2010, p.147) There are obviously many different components to each of the sectors in a city, but these three categories are helpful in identifying urban assets.

"The first sector we must consider is the *private* sector, composed of privately owned businesses, companies, corporations, small businesses, and banks which are not controlled by the state. These institutions are profit motivated" (Swanson & Williams, 2010, p.147-148). There are many followers of Jesus working and leading in the private sector in cities throughout the world. "The second sector is commonly referred to as the *public* sector. The public sector is that part of the economic and administrative life that deals with the delivery of goods and services by and for the government at the local, state, or national level. The public sector is owned by the state and exists to provide services that reflect the public interest. In some developed countries, these would include police and fire service, clean water and sanitation, and possibly waste management and garbage removal" (Swanson & Williams, 2010, p.148). The systems in the second sector are obviously a significant point of emphasis for the New Urban Agenda and the Sustainable Development Goals. "The third sector of every society is sometimes called just that – the *third* sector, or the *social* sector. It represents the wide range of community, voluntary, religious, and not-for-profit activities in society. The activities and programs of Christian churches would be included in this sector of society" (Swanson & Williams, 2010, p.148).

"In 1975, Campus Crusade for Christ founder Bill Bright and Youth With A Mission (YWAM) founder Loren Cunningham came together and identified what they called 'Seven Mountains of Influence' – pillars or domains of society that need to be transformed if the world is to be transformed. The seven mountains they identified were:

- Education: entities that engage in teaching and training
- Arts/Entertainment: entities that consciously produce or arrange sounds, colors, forms, movements, or other elements in a manner that affects the sense of beauty; entities that afford pleasure, diversion, or amusement
- Government: entities (local, regional, or federal) that serve the greater common good of society by restraining evil and promoting good
- Religion: religious or nonprofit service organizations, such as churches, synagogues, mosques, United Way, Boys & Girls Clubs, and so on
- Family: the fundamental social group in society, typically consisting of one or two parents and their children
- Media: entities that transmit information to the masses via radio, television, print, or the internet
- Business: enterprises that engage in the sale of goods or services" (Swanson & Williams, 2010, p.150).

These categories have been extremely helpful for many Christian leaders engaged in missional activity throughout the world. In my experience, these domains are especially helpful as followers of Christ develop strategic partnerships with other organizations in order to partner in working toward urban transformation.

Author Robert Linthicum describes three systems that are at work in cities. "First, there is the *political system*, that system which society makes decisions about its common life. Politics is simply the agreed-upon means by which society orders its life through the making of public and private decisions. The essential question of the political system is, how do we as a people determine to live together?" (Linthicum, 2003, p.23).

"Second, the *economic system* is that agreed-upon means by which a society's goods and services are generated and distributed. For all its complexity, economics is profoundly simple at its heart; it simply has to do with the way society agrees to generate and apportion wealth. The essential question of the economic system is, how do we as a people choose to create and distribute wealth?" (Linthicum, 2003, p.23). Many Christians are uncomfortable engaging the topic of money and economics, but there are so many incredible examples and so much powerful teaching on stewarding resources in order to bring about God's increasing levels of shalom throughout the Old and New Testaments in the Bible.

"Third, the *religious system* is a little more complex, but because of the predetermined meanings we bring to the word *religion*. The Latin root for the English *religion* simply means 'that which fences about.' In other words, what one believes sets the parameters around one's life. Our 'religion,' therefore, is the system which inculcates in a society the essential beliefs, values and basic convictions on which that society constructs its life together. The essential question of the religious system is, what do we, as a people, ultimately value?" (Linthicum, 2003, p.23). In this excellent book *Transforming Power*, Linthicum highlights how the religious system can have either a positive impact or a negative impact on the two other systems depending on how people steward the power that God provides.

During a lecture at a Doctor of Ministry course I took at Bakke Graduate University, Tim Svboda presented an effective model for city transformation. He presented a decentralized approach that seeks to identify systems, institutions, and people groups in cities that Christians in the city can impact through outwardly focused relationships. The ministry wheel, as he described it, has been an effective tool of urban transformation in the city of Chennai in India where he was engaged in ministry leadership for many years. Here are some examples of things discovered in cities that might be a part of a ministry wheel:

- Street kids
- Older adults
- Migrant workers
- Arts
- Education
- Persons with disabilities
- Business
- Government
- Drug addicts
- Universities
- Homeless population (Svboda, 2009, p.3).

Swanson and Williams note that Svboda's decentralized approach to city transformation fits nicely with the seven domains approach to understanding cities. "No longer should the church be the center of our thinking. Instead it is the Christians in the city, working and operating in their respective domains, who should be at the center of our thinking, with the church as one of the outer circles" (Swanson and Williams, 2010, p.152).

In his book *Encounter God in the City*, Dr. Randy White describes how Father Ben Beltran, a pastor in Manila, outlines the trinity of identity markers in cities. The three realities, symbolized by Latin terms, are the urbs, the civitas, and the anima. Dr. White notes that, "The urbs (from which we get our word *urban*) comprise the infrastructure of the city, including the physical layout, transportation systems, garbage collection, sewage, human interaction with the environment and so on… The *urbs* – the way a city is set up – influence the degree to which citizens benefit from a city's systems" (White, 2006, p.70).

Cities are not just systems and structures, though. "The *civitas* (from which we get our word civic) of a city has to do with its behaviors, its attitudes, its characteristics and its networks of people" (White, 2006, p.71).

Beyond the structures and behaviors of the people in a city, there is still a component of cities that really comes through when a person spends enough time there. "The *anima* of a city can be tricky to understand. It has to do with what Father Ben Beltran calls the 'unconscious universe' of the residents, the unspoken assumptions about God or about what governs and guides the people's existence. It often includes religious distinctives. Perhaps this is akin to what we might call the 'soul' of the city" (White, 2006, p.72).

Geographer Ronald R. Boyce notes that, "Cities are complex and compound. They are composed of a myriad of characteristics, each critical to understanding urbanism. The nature of cities is so vast and kaleidoscopic that it includes important components of many disciplines. Each discipline has its own perspective" (Boyce, 2009, p.5).

Just as Beltran put forward language to move beyond simple structures and systems to get to the heart of cities, Boyce presents six perspectives of the city that are helpful for working toward urban transformation. "*The Temporal Perspective* features the changing nature of cities and empires over time, diffusion over time and space, and model cities in history. *The Sacred Perspective* features temples, churches, mosques, sacred monuments, symbols of centrality and ethnocentricity, and the sacred nature of city sites. *The Security Perspective* features walls, gates, fortification, soldiers, strategically protected locations, law and order, empires, institutions, and emphasis on 'progress' – innovation. *The Economic Perspective* features markets, money, banks, exchange features, commerce, trade, and transportation, manufacturing, and promotion of tourism to gain money. *The Spatial Perspective* features the pattern of cities, intra-urban spatial display, sites of cities, and vertical vs. horizontal dimension balance. *The Social Perspective* features classes of people, community and governance – laws, monumental works of society, institutions – education, social, etc., and inter-personal and anonymous relationships" (Boyce, 2009, p.6).

I am sure that there are many more tools that would help people identify the signs of hope and assets in cities. Once the assets are identified in urban children and youth, and the assets are identified in cities, then urban Christian leaders interested in bringing about increasing levels of shalom need to focus on which strategies are most effective in complex urban environments.

Youth Development Models and Institutions

There are many effective youth development models that could be utilized to empower marginalized urban children such as after school programs, camping, child sponsorship, spiritual formation classes, sports ministries, counseling, tutoring, early childhood intervention, and drop in centers. Many city leaders take an institutional or systemic approach to impacting young people, including schools, youth detention centers, hospitals, orphanages, and churches.

In many countries around the world, Christian leaders are engaged at the macro level bringing about reform through systemic approaches and at the micro level through leadership in programs that reach children. What is the best approach? What works in cities? And, why should Christians be interested in best practices and what works in cities when it comes to transforming the lives of urban children and youth?

Why Should Christians Lead the Way?

Swanson and Williams note that, "While rural areas do have an effect on the culture of a nation or people group, there are at least six reasons why we need to engage cities at a deeper level;

1. Cites have a transforming effect on people.
2. Cities form a creative center.
3. Cities create fertile ground for thinking and receptivity.
4. Cities can help people live more efficiently and productively.
5. Cities are valued by God.
6. The early Christian movement was primarily urban" (Swanson & Williams, 2010, p.30).

Simply put, Christians need to engage in cities. Withdrawing from the messiness and complexities of urban life has proven not to be an effective response to rapid global urbanization. Rodney Stark emphasizes that, "All ambitious missionary movements are, or soon become, urban. If the goal is to 'make disciples of all nations,' missionaries need to go where there are many potential converts, which is precisely what Paul did" (Stark, 2006, p.26).

One of my mentors, Ray Bakke, points out that there are more than 1,250 verses related to cities in the Bible, so clearly cities are close to God's heart. And what about marginalized children and youth? Evangelical Christians should be leading the way based on God's heart for the fatherless described in Bible verses like;

> He executes justice for the fatherless and the widow, and loves the sojourner, giving him food and clothing.
>
> Deuteronomy 10:18 ESV

> [5]Father to the fatherless, defender of widows – this is God, whose dwelling is holy. [6]God places the lonely in families; he sets the prisoners free and gives them joy. But he makes the rebellious live in a sun-scorched land.
>
> Psalms 68:5-6 NLT

> Learn to do good. Seek justice. Help the oppressed. Defend the cause of the orphans. Fight for the rights of widows.
>
> Isaiah 1:17 NLT

> Religion that is pure and undefiled before God, the Father, is this: to visit orphans and widows in their affliction, and to keep oneself unstained from the world.
>
> James 1:27 ESV

There are many more passages of scripture that call Christians to lead the way when it comes to reaching children and youth, and today's children and youth are increasingly found in global urban environments. "God is doing something great in the earth, and the Lord is looking for leaders who will seize the day. God's kingdom is coming on earth, and it will unite people from every tribe and every nation, and God wants us to get involved with what is happening. As followers of our suffering Savior, we Christians are uniquely qualified to speak a word of reconciliation, a word of healing, a word of justice, and a word of grace to a world that is desperately in need of the Prince of Peace. God is calling each of us to the task" (McNeil, 2012, p.103).

Clearly, Christians are called to get involved, and many Christians have been engaged in work that is supposed to impact vulnerable children and youth. However, as Ash Barker discerned in *Slum Life Rising*, "Not all interventions in urban areas are effective. Many Christian aid organizations fail to emphasize urban strategies, and it can be hard to track and manage development work in urban slum and squatter neighborhoods" (Barker, 2012, Ch.3) His research found "the methodologies which have been successful in rural settings, like child sponsorships, have been less effective in urban slums" (Barker, 2012, Ch.3).

A great deal of research has been emerging about the ineffectiveness of many traditional development models, and as it relates to Christians, the ineffectiveness of the resources, time, and energy involved in short term mission trips with people from countries with lots of money visiting people in poorer countries. A lot more research needs to be done on the effectiveness of development programs and outreach efforts aimed at reaching urban children and youth who are experiencing poverty.

How effective are approaches to transforming the lives of high risk urban children and youth like child sponsorship, orphan care, partnerships, mentoring, sports/soccer, adoption, education reform, mass incarceration reform, health care, disease prevention and vaccinations, spiritual development, counseling, discipleship, parenting classes, early childhood intervention, the development of comprehensive social safety nets, government programs, after school programs, camping, initiation into adulthood, juvenile justice and incarceration, tutoring, faith-based partnerships, systemic and institutional reform, drop in centers, incarnational approaches, grass roots activism, and Christian Community Development?

And, how can followers of Christ be effect with impacting urban children and youth? A good place to start is with a healthy missional stance that Kris Rocke and Joel Van Dyke outline in *Geography of Grace*. "There are three primary missional prepositions. The first is 'to.' Ministries focusing on this proposition tend to locate power in very specific places such as the pulpit. They often deal with those they want to reach in a paternalistic manner; that is, they place themselves in a position of superiority over those they feel called to reach. Ministries that see 'mission' as something done to others may even become oppressive, violating the dignity and freedom of those to whom they minister in the name of Jesus" (Rocke & Van Dyke, 2012, p.74).

Ministry done *to* urban children and youth can cause a great deal of harm. But, so can another approach. "The second preposition is *for*. Rather than becoming paternalistic, these kinds of ministries can fall into the trap of being maternalistic. Many of us have grown up in families with well-meaning mothers who tried to do far more for us than was healthy. Many youth ministries, for example, tend to do far too many things for young people rather than equipping them to act on their own" (Rocke & Van Dyke, 2012, p.74). Running around doing a bunch of things for urban kids can ultimately lead to dependence, when what we should really be looking for is empowerment.

"A third missional prepositional option for the mission of the church is with. This is the incarnational preposition – *Immanuel* (God with us). When this preposition drives the mission, whether it's the church, organization, or even a short-term mission project, the potential to transform *both* the leaders *and* the people they seek to serve is heightened. Along with potential there is cost – these ministries require a much higher investment of time and relational energy (though much more is released in the long run)" (Rocke & Van Dyke, 2012, p.75). This approach involves going to where the urban children and youth are and spending time with them on their turf. It requires being present for long periods of time, asking good open ended questions, and excellent active listening skills. The incarnational approach is relationally focused on connecting adults and kids together in healthy ways. Kretzmann and McKnight point out "the most innovative community leaders are rediscovering that youth can be essential contributors to the well-being and vitality of the community. Projects that connect young people productively with other youth and adults are now seen to be the foundations upon which healthy communities can be built" (Kretzmann & McKnight, 1993, p.29). Amy Williams, who works with urban youth in Chicago, challenges people in the church to "See young people the way that God sees them. Young people are not a project to be fixed. We need to be able to see young people for their potential and not for their problems. We need to stop doing youth ministry to them and start doing it with them" (Hill, 2016).

Faith-based Mentoring

Research is beginning to show that mentoring relationships can significantly impact urban children and youth in positive ways. Mentoring relationships represent an integral approach to mission, connecting followers of Jesus in asset-building relationships with children, including informal, formal, community-based, school-based, and group mentoring methodologies. Faith-based mentoring describes the intentional placing of a caring adult from a congregation into a mentoring relationship with a high-risk young person. Faith-based mentors make at least a one-year commitment to see their mentee for several hours at a time each week.

Informal mentoring relationships occur more organically within the context of communities or extended families, while formal mentoring matches are intentionally established through a matching process that is usually facilitated by an organization for supervision purposes. Family-to-one mentoring provides the same kind of mentoring as one-to-one mentoring where an adult spends time with a child, except that a mentor's spouse and family are often deeply involved in the mentoring activities that take place at the mentor's home or out in the community. Group mentoring encompasses a group of caring adults who spend intentional and consistent time with a group of kids. Community-based mentors spend three or four hours each week with one mentee. The mentors make a minimum one-year commitment in which they will interact with a mentee out in the community, not in a school setting. Site-based mentoring, such as school-based mentoring, places one adult with one youth. The mentor makes a one-year commitment to spend at least two hours once a week with a mentee inside a school building or at a designated site rather that out in the community.

Transformational Mentoring

Transformational mentoring comprises intentional, long-term relationships between mentors and mentees that can lead to a process of transformation over time. Transformational mentoring relationships are calling, servant, and shalom-based; incarnational; reflective; contextual; global; and prophetic in nature. Many different definitions have been put forward, but I like Vinay Samuel's definition of transformation. "Transformation is to enable God's vision of society to be actualized in all relationships, social, economic, and spiritual, so that God's will may be reflected in human society and his love be experienced by all communities, especially the poor" (Samuel, 2016, p.215).

Transformational mentoring is a promising model of youth development that builds assets in urban children and youth. These mentoring relationships are also effective ways to connect urban kids to the assets in their cities. I would argue that when these eight perspectives on mentoring are present in a mentoring match between urban youth and Christian adults serving as mentors, transformation will occur in both mentors and mentees. And, with enough mentoring relationships in a city, increasing levels of shalom and thriving will emerge in cities.

Calling-based mentoring

Calling-based mentors commit to spending time with a mentee, despite the potential outcomes of the relationship, because mentoring is something that God has called them to see through to the finish. Called mentors stay in their matches longer because of their obedience to God. "The church universal… survives only by giving itself away. If you save your life, the Jesus principle goes, you will lose it. But if you lose it for my sake, then you will find it" (Lupton, 2005, p.214).

Rafael was referred to the mentoring program that I lead by several staff members at his school. When I first met him I noticed that he had significant anger issues, his grades were terrible, and he was extremely disruptive at school. He did not have a relationship with his father who was serving a life sentence in prison for murder. The other male influences in his life, his older brother and his uncle, were both heavily involved in gang activity and drug dealing. Mentoring Rafael was rough for the first couple of years. Sometimes we would connect and enjoy one another's company, and sometimes his anger would escalate and he would try to sabotage our relationship. He did not know how to respond to a positive male role model in his life, and I didn't really know how to respond to him. We both thought about ending the relationship many times. I stuck with this match because I knew God had called me to be Rafael's mentor.

Our relationship changed when Rafael accepted Christ. He was able to turn over a great deal of his pain and anger to the Lord, and I actually started to see a bright future for him. I could see Christ shining through in the midst of extreme brokenness. During our third year together, Rafael and his family had to flee the state because of his brother's drug debts. His brother and his uncle were murdered within one week of each other. When he moved back to Pittsburgh, the first phone call he made was to me. He started calling me every day, and I made sure to spend a lot of time with him considering everything he was going through. The time spent together was quite a strain, but it was something I was definitely called to do. God is slowly healing his heart, and I know God is working through me to reach him. If I viewed mentoring as just another program, then I am sure that I would have quit on Rafael long ago; however, I know that mentoring Rafael is much more than participation in a program to mentor high-risk youth. I have been called to build a long term relationship with him as one of the only positive male role models in his life. This meaningful relationship is indeed a high calling.

Contextual Mentoring

Contextual mentors respect a mentee's life and culture as they seek to help mentees experience meaning according to God's purposes, not from the perspective of a mentor's own limited worldview. These mentors help mentees to identify assets. "In the context of the poor, attentiveness to historical structures can be a means of acknowledging that individuals have some self-efficacy and control over their lives, despite being saddled with hardships and inequity" (Venkatesh, 2000, p.284). Contextual mentors could help mentees contribute back to their communities because many "young people yearn to contribute meaningfully to their community and can be seen to flourish when they are given the opportunity to do so" (Kretzmann & McKnight, 1993, p.30).

One of the boys I mentored happened to live on a street corner that experienced a high level of crime, including prostitution and drug dealing.

Every time he walked out his front door to go to school, to head to the YMCA, or hang out with friends, he was forced to walk right through the visual signs of addiction. He came from a big family with many siblings under one roof, but he was very resilient. When I first started spending time with him while he was in sixth grade, he was considered by his school to be at high-risk to drop out because he had demonstrated so many behavioral problems. He overcame the odds, though, to become a successful athlete and high school graduate.

Over the course of time, Steffon accepted Christ into his life; yet, he lived in a constant struggle to integrate his faith in Christ with the harsh realities of his life. I had a difficult time connecting him to a local church. He did not feel accepted entering into most churches. So, as a mentor, I served as one of the only Christians to speak regularly into Steffon's walk with Christ. We talked often about life and what it meant to follow Christ.

Contextualization was an important part of my role in Steffon's life. I continued to help him try to connect to a local church while I was discipling him. I was very careful to help him navigate through the struggles in his neighborhood. He learned to thrive at home, at school, and in his neighborhood that was filled with all kinds of illegal activity. I continued to encourage him in his relationship with Christ in culturally appropriate ways. That concept guided where I chose to take him during our time together, and how much time I chose to spend with him in his environment. Transformational mentors help their mentees to experience meaning in their own cultural contexts. These mentors help their mentees to orient their lives in God's story by experiencing the kingdom of God. "God's kingdom is not some amorphous, supra-cultural, other-world milieu. Rather, it is a space of vibrant, life-giving, God honoring encounter of spice and color, smell and sound, here and now, in the complex entanglement of human relations" (DeBorst, 2009, p.75-76).

Global Mentoring

Global mentors intentionally expand a mentee's worldview by teaching about the complexities of the modern world. Effective mentors may learn to understand the complex, global world and then pass that information onto their mentees. "If the church is to faithfully bear witness to the gospel in the global city, it must learn to understand the world and then find ways to creatively respond to it" (Gornik, 2002, p.204).

Derrick was a young man in a school-based mentoring program. During his transition from elementary school to middle school, I met with him weekly for lunch. Normally Derrick was a very outgoing child, so conversations with him were easy. We talked about the usual things that middle school boys talked about, such as girls, classes, girls, sports, girls, hip hop music, and more girls. I also made sure to keep up with what was going on with his family and home life.

Derrick started to open up about some significant issues that he was struggling with. In eighth grade he started to piece together his worldview. He made two comments to me in particular that stood out. First, he told me that he came to the realization that his neighborhood was a bad place with lots of violence and destruction. Second, he told me that he did not like being African-American.

Because of these deep issues that Derrick was bringing up to me, I decided that we needed to talk through his emotions. He was beginning to experience isolation that comes with living in poverty, so during our mentoring time together I began to help him dream about what kind of man he wanted to be some day. I did not want him to lose hope in his neighborhood, so I helped him to visualize himself contributing back to his own community. I also helped him to combat his isolation by dreaming about how he might make a difference in the world.

He loved to record himself making music. He made homemade videos for You Tube of him rapping, he entered several local rapping contests, and eventually he even started his own hip-hop group that went around the city doing concerts. I encouraged him to use his gifts globally. After all, who knows where God might lead him during his lifetime? I also talked to him about many amazing African-Americans who have made a tremendous difference in this world. It was easy for me to find good examples for us to discuss, and he became proud of his African-American ethnicity and heritage. It was important for me to help give him a global perspective on his life in order to combat his isolation and lack of self-esteem. Helping mentees to have a more global worldview leads to a more transformational mentoring experience.

Incarnational Mentoring

Incarnational mentors intentionally spend a significant amount of time with a mentee in the mentee's neighborhood or environment. These mentors enter into their mentee's environment in order to be more effective. Going into institutions like public schools to meet with students in order to participate in academic improvement is an example of what Ray Bakke calls common grace: "Common grace includes a transit system, a health-care system, an educational system, or a sewer system" (Bakke & Sharpe, 2006, p.113). Mark Gornik adds that incarnational mentors share hope with their mentees. "Hope proclaims – against all the relentless claims that a meaningful future is not possible, and against the constant agonies of suffering – that because of the cross and the resurrection, tomorrow can be different than today" (Gornik, 2002, p.234). As with the dangers associated with many incarnational approaches to ministry, mentors who spend a great deal of time with their mentees incarnationally need to avoid developing a savior complex by trying to do too much for them. "Mentors are naturally invested in making a difference in the lives of their mentee. However… mentors may become too involved in the life of the mentee and his or her family. Mentors who regularly visit the child's home, take siblings with them on outings, or try to solve family problems are putting your program, and themselves, at risk" (US Dept Education Mentoring Resource Center, 2006, p.3-4).

Tyran was essentially homeless when I first met him because he bounced around from house to house finding shelter with various friends and relatives. He is resourceful, resilient, creative, and he has a great outgoing personality that attracts people to him as a leader. In the past, Tyran has used those natural leadership skills in negative ways in order to meet his own needs. At one point in his life he sold drugs, stole property, and vandalized vacant buildings. He led other kids in the neighborhood to also get caught up in those things. Since Tyran spent so much of his childhood time walking around his neighborhood, and bouncing around between friends, he came into contact with many men who sought to involve him in leadership in local gangs. He had seemingly constant pressure on him to sell and use drugs.

When I first started mentoring Tyran, it was nearly impossible to keep up with him on a weekly basis. He missed a lot of school, so it was never a sure bet that he was going to be there on our mentoring days for me to pick him up. He did not have a cell phone, and there was no way to reach him by phone at any of the houses where he commonly slept. Dropping him off after the mentoring time was another significant challenge. He seemed to want to be dropped off at a different house every week. It has always been my practice as a mentor to make sure the mentees actually make it into their houses after I drop them off. Tyran would often be turned away from the houses where he asked me to try to take him. Eventually somebody would end up taking him in, but there was rarely any consistency in his life.

Two significant breakthroughs happened in my mentoring relationship with Tyran. First, he was able to get a cell phone so that when I needed to contact him he would be available to tell me where I could find him. It was still difficult to track him down, though, so the second breakthrough happened when I moved into his urban neighborhood. Tyran was now able to walk to my house, which helped tremendously in us being more consistent with spending time together. As an incarnational mentor, I also tried to be more intentional about finding him in his neighborhood and spending time with him there. We started utilizing the local YMCA as a place to hang out. My goal was simply to spend more time with Tyran in his context so that I could connect meaningfully with him more often. That strategy really paid off. He showed remarkable progress with his life. He did well in school, stayed out of trouble, and he accepted Christ into his life.

Having been in urban ministry for a while, I have learned that many people like to talk about the poor but few people are actually willing to give themselves away incarnationally to youth experiencing poverty in urban contexts. Information is not the issue. "The real issue is whether or not we as Christians are willing to be immersed in the concrete situations of the disenfranchised of our societies and witness to the lordship and saviorhood of Christ from within, a commitment that will have to be verified in our participation in the concrete transformation of these situations. Anything else is pure talk, and the kingdom of God 'does not consist in talk but in power.' (2 Cor. 4:20)" (Costas, 1982, p.16).

Prophetic Mentoring

Prophetic mentors provide mentees with a voice by advocating for them consistently over time. Prophetic mentors take on broken systems in a way that helps to clear the barriers to a mentee's development. Rhodes writes, "By bringing more privileged adults into the lives of less privileged young people, mentoring has the potential to promote widespread social change. Mentors' close personal connections with vulnerable youth afford them the opportunity to develop a first-hand understanding of the challenges faced by young people today, which can inspire them to redress social ills and advocate for social change that could improve the health and well-being of all youth living in these kinds of circumstances" (Rhodes, p.4). Christians have an important role to play in working toward justice in the lives of their mentees and in society in general. "The church's mission originates from God's mission and as such it must be broad enough to touch both the soul and the body, the society as well as the individual. It must have an impact on the people in their total need" (Chester, 2002, p.139).

One of the reasons I moved into the urban neighborhood where I lead a mentoring program was so I could support the many children who are on the waiting list for a mentor. I wish I had enough mentors for all of the children in the neighborhood who would like a mentor, but the needs are great and few people are called to become mentors. Nationwide in the United States, millions of children are waiting for a mentor so this problem is not unusual. Andre was one of those children. Andre had a school-based mentor through the mentoring program for one school year in fifth grade, but his mentor was unable to continue on and his match was closed. Since he really needed a positive adult influence in his life, he was added to the mentoring program waiting list. He lived about a block from my house, and he visited me many times. I informally mentored him because I saw him so much, and his older brother had a mentor through the program so I knew his family very well. His family lived on a dangerous block that experienced gunshots on a seemingly daily basis.

Andre and two other boys from the waiting list who often visited our house were arrested and charged with felony assault for beating up and robbing a man. When Andre was arrested, his family was very distraught. His older brothers sought retribution against the families of the other two boys who were arrested, and as a family friend and a pastor in the community I spent time with them over at their house to try to deescalate the situation. The efforts worked for the time being, but the situation on their block became very intense.

I went to court with Andre's mom, and while we were waiting she mentioned to me that they had been assigned a public defender but that person had not returned her many phone calls to meet with her before the trial. The trial was set for that day, and Andre and his mom met with their assigned lawyer for just a few minutes before going into the courtroom. He convinced Andre to plead guilty to the same deal as the two other boys even though he had not participated in the actual crime (according to Andre he was just walking with the boys who committed the crime).

I tried to advocate as best as I could for Andre and his mom, but it seemed the entire legal system was against them. All three boys, these kids who I knew well from my neighborhood and had shared meals with at my dining room table many times, were sentenced to be removed from their homes in order to serve time in the youth detention system.

Having served as a mentor for Andre even though we were not officially matched, I was troubled about his experience in what appeared to me to be a broken legal system. His legal representation was terrible. He may have deserved legal consequences for being present when a crime occurred, but I was disheartened by the harsh legal process his family endured. Andre's negative experience has caused me to become a passionate advocate for judicial system and incarceration reform, in cases where they particularly impact minority urban youth.

Prior to the time of his arrest, I had spoken frequently into Andre's life. His future seemed to be clouded with gang activity, violence, jail, or death. I had often encouraged him to stay in school, focus on the positive things in his life, while casting a powerful, Christ-centered focus for his future. Even though this negative outcome occurred in his life, I continued to speak truth to him whether he was in jail or not. I have also made many efforts to reform the broken legal system that so negatively impacts people I care about like Andre.

Prophetic mentors speak truth into their mentees lives, and they advocate for their mentees when systems let them down. Those dysfunctional systems could be legal, educational, economic, or others, but it is important for transformational mentors to advocate for their mentees individually and systematically if needed depending on the circumstances. "Advocacy begins the process of restoring creation to shalom. When we are willing to advocate for or stand up and speak in defense of another person, God can use our words to end the injustice against that person" (George & Toyama-Szeto, 2015, p.103).

Reflective mentoring

Reflective mentors move beyond programs and activities and focus their mentoring experiences in a way that will allow them and their mentee to find meaning within the context of their relationship. Mentors could arrive at transformation in their lives and in their mentees' lives through reflection. "The goal of the church's holistic outreach is the transformation of people, communities, and society for the glory of God. For God to work through us in this mission requires that we first, and continually, allow him to transform us" (Sider, Olson & Unruh, 2002, p.142). Sometimes adults fall into relationships with young people that are inauthentic, usually as a result of something called "adultism." "A powerful underlying reason for non-authentic youth engagement is adultism – the behavior and attitudes that flow out of negative stereotypes adults hold about young people. Adultism is rooted in the belief that young people lack intelligence or ability. This belief is strongly supported by societal norms which leave young people feeling that they are not valued, respected, or heard. Even adults who deeply care for young people may have internalized these misconceptions and may not be aware that they are behaving in an adultism manner" (ACT for Youth Center for Excellence).

Just like any group of people in society, high-risk youth have a wide variety of unique personalities. Hence, some mentees are extremely outgoing; some are extremely introverted, and others are every other type of personality in between. Andrew is an example of a mentee who happens to be extremely extroverted. He talks a lot, and when he is with a group he is usually the conversation starter and center of attention. One of Andrew's best friends, Tyree, is introverted. He does not talk very much, although every once in a while in a group setting he will jump in with a comment. I served as a school-based mentor to Andrew and Tyree. I tried to be intentional about spending one-on-one mentoring time with each of them, but I also spent time with them together during lunch at their school.

Reflection was a crucial component of the time that I spent with both

Andrew and Tyree. Since Andrew is outgoing, he verbally processed through the experiences that happened in his life. If he was having family problems or struggles with his relationships at school, when he spent time with me he just started running on and on about those issues. I listened to what he was saying, and I helped him to reflect on what he was dealing with in his life. I asked him reflective questions that made him think more deeply. We often stumbled upon teachable moments when I practiced reflective mentoring with him. On the other hand, if I did not pay attention during my time with Tyree we would probably go months without having any meaningful reflection about life. I asked him open-ended questions to help him reflect about the meaning of the things he experienced. These quality mentoring moments can only be discovered with purposeful intentionality on the part of the mentor. If I viewed our relationship as simply a program or a way to give back to the community as many mentoring programs do, I might have become frustrated with both of these mentoring matches and given up prematurely. Instead I discovered that proactive reflective mentoring leads to a more transformational mentoring experience for both mentors and mentees.

Beyond helping mentees to reflect, it is also important for mentors to reflect on how the mentoring experience is transforming their own lives. When mentors give time to others in service for Christ, they are stretched in many good ways. Without reflection, mentors might become overwhelmed by the match pressures. Although mentors should not try to control the outcomes of the match, mentors can be more or less effective depending on their own consistent behavior over time. Just as with any long-term relationship, change is necessary over time. Reflective mentors navigate the ever-changing dynamics of mentoring relationships with high-risk youth because they regularly assess how they are connecting with their mentee.

Servant Mentoring

Servant mentors initially become involved in mentoring because they want to serve God; however, as a result they come to be of service to a mentee. "People of faith reach out to others because they have received divine love and they share it with others in gratitude. Those who do so enter into a reciprocal relationship that changes not only the person who receives, but also the one who gives" (Elliot, 2004, p.255). Servant mentors share their lives with their mentees because "The Christian life envisions a communal life" (Dahm, 2004, p.68). Servant mentors are able to stand the test of time. "Unlike many forms of volunteering – such as cleaning up a neighborhood or helping with an event – the impact of mentoring is not seen immediately... Because mentoring relationships take time to gain momentum, it is critical that mentors have patience and the ability to work through any difficult stretches" (US Dept of Education Mentoring Resource Center, 2006).

Catrell was the first mentee I was matched with in the mentoring program that I currently lead. He had shown some signs of being somewhat disruptive at his school, so the staff recommended him to the program. For our first few months together, I was actually wondering why he needed a mentor. His grades seemed to be good, and his behavior was not too bad relative to some of the other boys I had met him at his school. We then met every week over the summer, and one of the things I noticed was that he never thanked me for spending time with him. When I would drop him off at his apartment, he would just get out of the car and walk to his house without ever looking back.

When the school year started, I actually thought that my influence on him was making him worse. He was suspended for nine days during that fifth grade year of school, and his grades dropped dramatically from what they had been before he was matched with me. I was not sure if he would want to go on for another year when it came time for our one-year celebration. I did not know if he enjoyed our time together because he rarely showed any kind of appreciation. Still, I didn't feel released from our match. God had called me to mentor Catrell, and as a servant of the Lord I was called to serve him with my time and energy. The second year of the match was even worse. His grades dropped even more, and he was in danger of being held back because of the number of days he had been suspended. I still could not tell if he even liked having a mentor. I felt like a failure.

At one point during our third year together, Catrell got into a fight while playing laser tag with one of the other boys in the mentoring program. I had to take him home, and on the car ride to his house I remember thinking that it was not worth it to mentor him anymore. It was just too much trouble. He was very upset with me for taking him home after the fight, and he kept telling me, "I hate you. I hate this mentoring program. I never want to see you again." When we got to his house, he slammed the car door and stormed into his house. I called my mentoring supervisor to explain what had happened, and I informed her that this was probably the end of the match. It was apparent to me that Catrell did not want anything to do with this relationship. In my mind, mentoring him was a thankless task and it was only making him worse, anyway. A funny thing happened. The mentoring supervisor disagreed with me. She told me that as a follower of Christ, I should die to myself and allow Christ to shine through me. She told me to serve Catrell by showing up the following week to pick him up, so that's exactly what I did. He was completely shocked when I arrived to pick him up, and we talked briefly about what had happened the previous week. He apologized, and we went out together for our mentoring time. It was one of the best mentoring times we ever had together.

During our third year together, Catrell's grades and behavior at school improved dramatically. He turned things around and went on to graduate from one of the most academically rigorous high schools in the city. He still rarely thanked me for the time that we spent together, but I was completely fine with that. God called me to serve Catrell even if I did not get much out of the relationship early on. I know that the mentoring benefited him. If I were simply volunteering in a mentoring program, I might have given up on the relationship with Catrell long ago. Instead, as a servant mentor, God worked through me to make the mentoring match a more transformational experience.

Shalom Mentoring

Shalom mentors are bridge-builders who encourage reconciliation between a mentee and the world around them. Fikkert and Corbett offer that the, "goal is to see people restored to being what God created them to be: people who understand that they are created in the image of God with the gifts, abilities, and capacity to make decisions and to effect change in the world around them; and people who steward their lives, communities, resources, and relationships in order to bring glory to God. (Fikkert & Corbett, 2009, p.81). Faith-based mentoring leads to increasing levels of shalom in struggling urban communities.

Shortly after the church where I serve as a pastor began partnering with a local urban school district to provide mentors to children attending public schools, the school district made some difficult decisions to close several schools in order to adjust to the declining enrollment in the district. One of the school closures dramatically impacted the neighborhood where the mentoring program was located. Children attending a school in a nearby neighborhood had their school close, and were forced to attend the school where the mentoring program was located.

There was a lot of controversy in the decision to join the schools together because of community and gang rivalries. Safety became a concern. The first couple of weeks were very difficult, just as the communities had feared. Old rivalries ran deep, and students fought each other going to and from school, and while they were at school. I tried to remain present there as much as possible to help out in any way that I could, but the problems were many and the staff at the school were overwhelmed. The school was not a safe environment. As I reflected on the situation,

I thought that there might be a way for the mentors from our church to make a difference. I asked the staff to give me the names of the five boys in the youngest middle school grade that were causing the most problems in terms of class disruption and fighting. I set up a group mentoring program with the boys in which I matched each one of them up with a one-to-one mentor, and we met every Thursday after school for four hours. Sometimes we stayed at school for different group activities that I had planned such as science experiments or playing basketball in the gym, and sometimes we went off campus to visit museums or sporting events. We always had food and fun as our two main components.

At first it was nearly impossible to get all five boys there at the same time. We initially only had one or two boys show up, and it was usually different boys each time. Inevitably, several of the boys were suspended from school or they would just not attend the program. After a couple of months, we finally started getting the boys to come consistently, but when they came they often fought with one another. They were from competing gang territories based in different parts of both neighborhoods. These boys did not like each other, and outbursts of escalated anger were common in the group.

The mentors were very patient with the boys during that first year, and when everyone showed up to work with the mentees for a second year they were stunned. However, we noticed something change during our second year together. The boys were starting to get along with one another, and they were starting to become leaders in the school to help create a more positive climate. These high-risk young men from violent neighborhoods with competing gangs went from hating each other to being best friends. In fact, they were almost inseparable. To this day, they remain very good friends. They stayed out of trouble and became leaders during the rest of their time at the school and throughout high school. They became leaders and agents of reconciliation in their families and neighborhoods. To observe and participate in that transformation was remarkable. I continue to have high hopes for all of the young men now that they are adults.

The group mentoring experience that I just described is an example of how ordinary mentors can become shalom mentors. This type of mentoring becomes a transformational experience when mentors commit to helping their mentees become reconcilers across cultures and even across rivalries within communities. Isolation mixed with deep-rooted anger can lead to violence, but intentionally building positive relationships with different people helps to build the capacity for peace and health in struggling urban communities. Transformational mentors intentionally integrate the concept of shalom into the fabric of their match through planned activities and shared experiences. Reconciliation is the key. "The goal of reconciliation is not to persuade or be persuaded, but rather to understand and to be understood and respected. The more we understand and respect across lines of culture and ethnicity, the more we will be able to bring together people of all races and cultures into the one worshiping body of Christ and to develop the communities in which we live" (Gordon & Perkins, 2013, p.67).

Positive Outcomes, Barriers, and Opportunities

While transformational mentoring shows many positive signs of impacting urban children and youth, it is important to note that there is no one-size-fits-all approach to the process of transformation. A young person may grow in assets, and become connected to the assets in their city, and still need counseling to overcome trauma or may benefit from a Christian camping experience or tutoring program. It should all work together with a lot of collaboration by Christians who are engaged in many different spheres of influence.

Yes, mentoring can lead to holistic growth and reconciliation across age, racial, ethnic, and cultural barriers. But, there are also barriers to establishing and sustaining long term mentoring relationships. Sometimes urban youth or mentors move too far away from each other to keep the relationships going. In some cities, the gap between rich and poor is so big that mentors with access to resources could literally be kidnapped and held for ransom if they risked going into a poor urban neighborhood to pick up a mentee. Often partnership dynamics between organizations change as leaders transition and funding sources dry up. It's hard work to overcome many of the barriers. Healthy, long term mentoring relationships that lead to a process of transformation require commitment, consistency, and compassion.

Still, the future looks bright for mentoring. The New Urban Agenda and the Sustainable Development Goals can be achieved, and urban children and youth can contribute to the process of empowerment as their assets are built and as they are connected to the assets in their city through meaningful relationships. Christians can lead the way, and the process of transformation in our cities will happen one life at a time.

References

Bakke, R. & Sharpe, S. (2006). *Street Signs: A New Direction in Urban Ministry* Birmingham, AL: New Hope Publishers.

Barker, A. (2012). *Slum Life Rising: How To Enflesh Hope Within a New Urban World*. Kindle Edition

Chester, T. (2002). *Justice, Mercy, and Humility*. Waynesboro, GA: Paternoster Press.

Costas, O. (1982). *Christ Outside the Gate: Mission Beyond Christendom* Maryknoll, NY: Orbis.

Dahm, C. (2004). *Parish Ministry in a Hispanic Community*. Mahwah, NJ Paulist Press.

Elliott, B. (2004). *Street Saints: Renewing American Cities*. West Conshohocken PA: Temple Foundation Press.

Fikkert, B. & Corbett, S. (2009). *When Helping Hurts: How to Alleviate Poverty Without Hurting the Poor... and Ourselves.* Chicago, IL: Moody Publishers.

George, A. & Toyama-Szeto, N. A. (2015). *God of Justice.* Downers Grove, IL: InterVarsity Press.

Gordon, W. & Perkins, J.M. (2013). *Making Neighborhoods Whole: A Handbook for Christian Community Development.* Downers Grove, IL: InterVarsity Press.

Gornik, M. (2002). *To Live in Peace: Biblical Faith and the Changing Inner City.* Grand Rapids, MI: William B. Eerdmans Publishing.

Kretzmann, J.P. & McKnight, J.L. (1993). *Building Communities from the Inside Out: A Path Toward Finding and Mobilizing a Community's Assets.* Skokie, IL: ACTA Publications.

Linthicum, R. (2003). *Transforming Power: Biblical Strategies for Making a* Difference in Your Community. Downers Grove, IL: InterVarsity Press.

Lupton, R. (2005). *Renewing the City: Reflections on Community Development and Urban Renewal.* Downers Grove, IL: InterVarsity Press.

Padilla DeBorst, R. (2009). 'Unexpected' Guests at God's Banquet Table: Gospel in Mission and Culture. *Evangelical Review of Theology.* 33(1), 75-76.

Rocke, K. & Van Dyke, J. (2012). *Geography of Grace: Doing Theology From Below.* Tacoma, WA: Street Psalms Press.

Ruthruff, R. (2010). *The Least of These: Lessons Learned from Kids on the Street.* Birmingham, AL: New Hope Publishers.

Salter-McNeil, B. (2012). In A. Tizon (Ed). *Missional Preaching: Engage, Embrace, Transform.* Valley Forge, PA: Judson Press.=

Samuel, V. (2016) in G. Hill, *Global Church: Reshaping Our Conversations, Renewing Our Mission, Revitalizing Our Churches.* Downers Grove, IL: InterVarsity Press.

Sider, R., Olson, P. & Unruh, H. (2002). *Churches that Make a Difference: Reaching Your Community with Good News and Good Works.* Grand Rapids, MI: Baker Books.

Stark, R. (2006). *Cities of God: The Real Story of How Christianity Became an Urban Movement and Conquered Rome*. New York, NY: Harper One.

Swanson, E. & Williams, S. (2010). *To Transform a City: Whole Church, Whole Gospel, Whole City*. Grand Rapids, MI: Zondervan

Tutu, D. (1999). *No Future Without Forgiveness*. New York: Doubleday.

Venkatesh, S. (2000). *American Project: The Rise and Fall of a Modern Ghetto*. Cambridge, MA: Harvard University Press.

West, C. (1993). *Race Matters*. New York: Vintage Books

White, R. (2006). *Encounter God in the City: Onramps to Personal and Community Transformation*. Downer's Grove, IL: InterVarsity Press.

Websites

ACT for Youth Center for Excellence. *Authentic Youth Engagement*. Retrieved October, 2016, from http://www.actforyouth.net/youth_development/authentic.cfm.

Rhodes, J. *Research Corner: Ethical Principles for Youth Mentoring Relationships*. Retrieved October, 2016, from http://www.mentoring.org/downloads/mentoring_1335.pdf.

Search Institute. *40 Development Assets for Adolescents (Ages 12-18)*. Retrieved October, 2016, from www.search-institute.org.

The Stanford Center on Poverty and Inequality, (2009). *20 Facts About U.S. Inequality That Everyone Should Know*. Retrieved October, 2016, from www.stanford.edu/group/scspi/cgi-bin/facts.php.

UNICEF, *Child info: Monitoring the Situation of Children and Women, "Orphan Estimates."* Retrieved October, 2016, from http://www.childinfo.org/hiv_aids_orphanestimates.php.

Williams, A. (2016). A Hope Dealer: Urban Youth Ministry Today. In G. Hill, *The Global Church Project Podcast – Episode 35*. Retrieved October, 2016, from, http://theglobalchurchproject.com/wp-content/uploads/2016/10/Williams-Full-Interview.mp3.

Other Resources

Boyce, R.R. (2009). *The Essence of Cities* (lecture notes and article overview). Seattle, WA: Bakke Graduate University.

Office of the Assistant Secretary for Planning and Evaluation (2014). *Information on Poverty and Income Statistics: A Summary of 2014 Current Population Survey Data.* Retrieved October, 2016, from http://aspe.hhs.gove/14/PovertyAndIncomeEst/ib_poverty2014.pdf.

Svboda, T. (2009). *Overture I Lecture Notes* (course notes). Seattle, WA: Bakke Graduate University.

UN General Assembly, *Resolution Adopted by the General Assembly on 25 September 2015.*

UN Habitat, (2016). *The New Urban Agenda.* October 2016. Quito: Ecuador

U.S. Department of Education Mentoring Resource Center. (2006). *Mentoring Fact Sheet: Managing Risk After the Match is Made.*

U.S. Department of Education Mentoring Resource Center. (2006). *Mentoring Fact Sheet: Overcoming Relationship Pitfalls.*

U.S. Department of Housing and Urban Development. *United States of America National Report for the Third United Nations Conference on Housing and Sustainable Development (Habitat III).*

Urban Shalom - Seeing People & Community with New Eyes

7

Mary Nelson

One of the gifts of the UN Habitat III gathering, was the *Cities We Need document – Toward a New Urban Paradigm*. It was put together by the World Urban Campaign in preparation for the Quito 2016 UN event. It highlights ten principles for a new urban paradigm which include not only the physical planning and shape of the cities we need, but also the way in which people live together, the basics of community and the foundations of justice and equity;

The city we need;

1. is socially inclusive and engaging
2. is affordable, accessible and equitable
3. is economically vibrant and inclusive
4. is collectively managed and democratically governed
5. fosters cohesive territorial development
6. is regenerative and resilient
7. has shared identities and sense of place
8. is well planned, walkable and transit-friendly

9. is safe, healthy and promotes wellbeing
10. learns and innovates

The Cities We Need principles are aligned with but bring a broader scope to the eight key components of the Christian Community Development Association's philosophy of approach. In short the philosophy focuses on

- Redistribution of resources
- Relocation to live amongst those we work with
- Reconciliation of people to God and each other
- Leadership development of those in poor neighborhoods
- Empowerment of individuals
- A holistic approach to working with individuals and communities
- Being church based
- Listening to the community

This broader scope includes the physical environment, and aspects like transportation and a commitment to communities becoming economically vibrant and inclusive (Principle 7). They also include governance issues working for cities to become collectively managed and democratically governed (principle 4). This wider vision of community beyond the neighborhood is an important addition to the CCDA focus which has traditionally been on a given neighborhood and the people within it.

So often we as Christians approach underserved communities with a "we have come to serve you, we have come to save you" attitude. That is self-defeating in the long haul. We bring in programs that need funding only for them to run out of steam when the funding dies out. Such an approach denies community people dignity, creates dependency and often leads to ill-conceived efforts. Bob Lupton, in *Toxic Charity*, shares how demeaning it is, when we as good suburban Christians give Christmas baskets to an inner-city family. He goes on to describe alternatives that uphold the dignity of people (Lupton, 2011). Brian Fickkert in *When Helping Hurts*, shows how often our service trips, our mission trips from resourced countries to under-resourced places often do more harm than good. Groups come digging wells that include machines local people do not know how to fix or have access to parts. This has a demoralizing impact on community residents, with outsiders coming in to "fix things" rather than using a bottom up approach (Corbet and Fickkert, 2014).

The same is true of our churches and faith-based organizations in under-served communities. Communities First (Von Gronnigan) describes three kinds of churches in under-resourced areas;

1. Church "in" the community (Fortress) where there are locked doors which are only open when there are services. The focus is people coming into the building;
2. Church "to" the community (Savior) where programs are operated around what the church thinks the people need;
3. Church "with" the community (partner), where initiatives emerge from listening to the people and identifying how the Church can walk alongside and support community initiatives.

This last approach can often be messy and take time, but it is the most effective way to empower and strengthen the community.

We are reminded of the words of Micah 6:8 (NKJV) "What does the Lord require of you, but to do justly, to love mercy and to walk humbly with your God?" Walking humbly is the hardest part for many of us. However, humility lets us listen to the people, helps us to take an accompanying role rather than the leadership role, and helps us admit our mistakes.

When working with a local community, so often we start with a needs assessment, the needs of people and place, and therefore see little of the possibilities and opportunities. This distorts our whole approach and leaves the people and community deemed "needy" waiting for outsiders such as the government, the church, etc. to come to their rescue. This creates a sense of hopelessness; the problems are too big; there is no hope.

The City We Need vision for the cities of the future gives rise to hope and aspiration. It provides aspirational goals, and a set of guidelines for action. Likewise, Isaiah 65:17-25 (TEV) shares God's vision of the New

Creation, a city "full of joy and happy people. Babies will no longer die in infancy…. people will build houses and get to live in them….. they will enjoy the things they have worked for." When we work in community, we need God's vision for what can happen, of what "beloved community" looks like. Add that to the specific vision and hopes of the people in the community and one finds energy to move forward.

So, we need a new set of eyeglasses to look at under resourced people and place. So often people in our communities are labeled poor, drug dependent, gang bangers, generally dependent, and only seen by their labels. So often, we (who are educated, who are Christian, who have experience) think we have the answers. But the eyeglasses of faith help us to "listen to the people" and uncover the gifts, talents, assets and hopes of labeled people in our communities.

It takes intentionality to see the opportunities in place of the liabilities, to identify the gifts and talents of people, the resources of a community. In Asset Based Community Development (ABCD) we talk about the glass that is half full/half empty. Too often our needs assessments start with the glass half empty and we work from there. This leads to the community needing outside help.

Instead, we should start with the glass being half full, the gifts and talents, hopes and energies of people in the community. It's called an asset inventory. Get a group of people to think about the gifts and talents they have... gifts of the heart, gifts of the head, gifts of the hands. Gifts of the heart like listening skills, empathy, compassion. Gifts of the head like planning and organizing, like strategy and alternatives. Gifts of the hands like cooking, carpentry, painting, music. I have never found a group of individuals who were labelled poor or unskilled or gangbangers or elderly, etc, that when given time to identify their gifts (or asked what would your best friend say are your gifts?) failed to come up with a room full of talents and gifts. These are the building blocks of community development.

Another tool for getting at the strengths and assets of people and community, is getting people to share their stories... stories of when the community was functioning best, stories when they experienced "beloved community", stories of special people in their lives. One of the CCDA principles is "Listening to the Community." So often we with education and experience want to do too much of the talking, and don't really listen. Sometimes effective listening is simply in the form of presence. I am reminded of the story of some Bishops who came to inspect a devastated oceanfront community, and as they were leaving, saw an old woman sitting on a bench with the backdrop of her destroyed shack behind her. A Bishop said to her, "We are from the Church, and we want to help. How can we help you?" She looked at him and quietly said, "Come sit with me." Building community means listening to the community, hearing the stories and sometimes sitting in quietude with someone.

Along with discovering the assets of individuals comes the identification of what people see and want in their community. We have used the approach of community members going out two by two to talk with their neighbors in a defined area. Three basic questions are asked:

1. What are the two or three best things about this community?
2. What are the two or three things that need working on?
3. Which of these are you interested in working on?

Out of this process comes both the community's identification of initiatives that can become collective efforts, and identifies the people interested in working on them. It is important that at this stage smaller efforts are identified. For example, in one community some people said there was a lot of trash in the community and they were willing to work on it. This led to a "clean up green up" day; kids helped, adults organized trash bins and sorting, and seniors cooked food to reward the workers at the end of the day. Key outcomes were visible results, and an experience of community.

A part of this process is making sure there is intentional indigenous leadership development from within the community (one of the principles of CCDA). This takes identifying the local leaders that share a vision and including them in the opportunity to learn more, attend the conferences, take opportunities to lead with the freedom to make mistakes, but with behind the scenes support to make it work.

An ancient Chinese poem, used by CCDA as a basic frame of understanding of this process reflects the principles mentioned above.

Go to the people
Live among them
Learn from them
Love them
Start with what they know
Build on what they have;
But of the best leaders
When their task is done
The people will say,
"We have done it ourselves."

It is important to note the process of getting to empowerment. Proximity. Living among them, learning from them (respect for their culture, ideas, ways), and finally getting to love them. Then starting with what is there, what they know and have.

We are reminded of the Five Loaves and Two Fishes in the Gospel of John (6:1-14). First of all, Jesus SAW the multitude and knew of their need for food. In response to Jesus's concern to feed them, the disciples looked for a commercial approach, there was not enough money, only the sense of scarcity. When the disciples identified what was there in the crowd, a little boy with five loaves and two fishes, it seemed like a drop in the bucket. But Jesus took what was there, and made it enough, with some left over. The abundance of God's work.

In one low income community, the faith based organization did an asset inventory in the quest to create jobs. They discovered the community had a lot of natural caregivers, people who were already caring for family or neighbors, etc. It also discovered the "age wave", that people were living longer and care for the elderly as a type of work had a bright future. So, matching these two, the organization identified community people interested in this work, and then sought a contract to provide the services to the elderly in the wider community. Jobs were created, people were paid for caring for neighbors (at much less cost than institutional care). Several years later, understanding that these were not living wage jobs, the organization joined others in advocating for rates that enabled living wages. One thing leads to another.

Looking with new eyes at a community includes "asset mapping," the process of community people identifying the physical aspects of their community such as rivers, parks, garbage dumps, churches, schools, wells, government institutions, hospitals, vacant land, transportation (or lack of). This includes identifying the connections to other resources and situations outside the community but related to it. Then, people can see what is there with new eyes.

There is an example where asset mapping in an Indian community which had suffered from flooding helped the village determine water flow, where gardens should be replanted, and where houses should be located to keep them safe.

One of the examples coming out of the Urban Habitat III experience was Ecuadoran government planners sharing their work of turning a recent devastation of the flooding of a whole village into an opportunity to think creatively, rebuilding it with energy efficient, sustainable and transit related development.

Here are some other examples of new eyes seeing opportunities. In Chicago, a faith based organization did asset mapping and identified a lot of garbage, including automobile tyres. So, they explored recycling opportunities, and decided to establish a cash buy back center, with minimal equipment and opportunity to hire returning citizens from prison who had difficulty finding jobs. The cash buy back provided people, especially at the end of the month when cash was short, money to supplement their incomes. The center provided jobs for people who were able to use them as a stepping stone to a better life. And it helped to clean up the environment.

In East Timor, people in a very poor urban community "saw" all the abandoned automobile tyres and experimented with creating chairs out of the tires. That led to a number of enterprises, including making shoes and other things from the tyres. New Eyes to see help even very poor communities capture new opportunities, and start to move into action.

There is no magic in this approach to community development. It starts from the inside out, with small, local efforts that can be accomplished with local resources in the shorter term. The community's eyes are then open to larger efforts that require bringing local initiative and resources together with outside resources, whether that be church associations, government or other not-for-profits. But in coupling the local efforts with larger efforts, one has to be careful that the local leadership does not get submerged.

So often, however, there are setbacks and disappointments. When these occur we need to pause what we are doing and organize with others for action around the policies and efforts that are hindering community advancement. An old community saying goes, "Don't agonize, organize." That's also where the inspiration and "gasoline" of our faith and the faith community comes in.

As people of a faith community, we have access to some special power. call it the three "g's." First, the "glue" of God's call to be about the work of justice and community that binds us together despite ageism, racism and economic gaps. Next, the "gasoline" for the long haul. God's call renews us and gives us new energy. Often, we come depressed and disappointed to pray, and God lifts up our spirits and gives us new energy to try again to find another way. And finally, it's the "guts" to make the risky decisions to put our lives on the line for justice and community.

In the beginning of one community's efforts to build affordable housing in a broken down neighborhood, the Church sought a bank loan and the bank asked for collateral. There was nothing in the bank accounts, no wealthy friends. They then realized that they owned their little church building free and clear of any debt. There was the collateral! They held a congregational church meeting to approve mortgaging the church, the one thing they owned. It was risky to mortgage the building to do low income housing in the neighborhood. Congregants shared their fears. Then an older lady in the church got up and said, "We just gotta do it. People will see something happening in the community, and the church as the instigator." The mortgage was approved. It was a win-win situation. The bank knew that the church would do whatever was needed to make sure the loan was repaid, and the church people knew that if the bank dared try to foreclose on the church, they would be there picketing the bank with signs.

Another one of the insights from the UN Habitat III and Cities We Need documents is the connection between the neighborhood and the systems of cities such as transportation. A Westside Chicago community, empowered by the church organization, joined with other environmental groups to protest the closing down of the elevated train line that connected the community to downtown, the Southside and the suburbs. It was the transportation to jobs (for a community where many people did not have cars), to health care, to families and friends. The community joined together with Greenpeace and the Transit Riders Association and together they attended the meetings. It discovered in the process of saving the transit line, that a transit stop (with a liquor store and currency exchange and boarded up buildings) could be a major community asset. The group got assistance and financing from outside and developed a smart, green (energy efficient) building at the intersection. It became a transit oriented development with child care, a bank, and employment center. That development spurred the building of energy efficient houses in walking distance of the stop.

What can Christians in Mission learn from the Cities We Need and UN Habitat III efforts?

Too often in our neighborhood ministries we get tunnel vision and focus only on the immediate aspects of our neighborhood and forget that the systems of the city, the broader environment have major impact on the lives and sustainability of our neighborhoods. So, we need to understand the relationships between these factors, we need to understand the various systems (transportation, water, land, etc) in order to add our voice and impact to the directions and formulations of these systems. For example, access to public transportation is critical for people and employment. Access to clean water is critical for life. The struggle of so many indigenous communities around the right and access to clean water in the face of encroaching pipelines raised consciousness around the world. "Water is Life" became the mantra. We have too often taken basic aspects of the environment in our communities for granted.

Christians have only recently become more engaged in the environmental movement. Some have denied climate change, even as whole islands are being wiped out with the rise of ocean waters due to huge hunks of artic ice falling away. We need to revamp what we are doing in light of our need to live as stewards of God's creation. This impacts how we use energy, how we despoil or save clean water, how we recycle and reuse what is there, how we curb our drive for material well being over what's sustainable and needed.

So where does the church fit into the Cities We Need?

Al Barett, Vicar of Hodge Hill Church in Birmingham, England, wrote "Asset-Based Community Development: a Theological Reflection." He points out three aspects.

1. ABCD is asset-based, discovering and celebrating what's already there. He says: ABCD invites us to open our eyes to the ways God has blessed this place and this people with goodness, vitality and fruitfulness. It

may be in the place itself, in the stories that it contains or in the webs of relationships that knit it together. It certainly begins by recognizing the wealth of gifts o the people who inhabit it have and the marks of the "image of God" that define each and every one of them."

2. ABCD builds communities from the 'inside out': being present with others. "It starts with the lowest level of interaction between neighbors and helps to grow networks and associations that, in time, discover the power to make change happen through acting together." In this sense, it is a challenge to the power of money. Money claims it is the way to develop communities. We claim that building associations, creating common bonds, sharing in action is the way to create communities. ABCD also challenges the way that government and the market "asset strip" certain neighborhoods, while it proclaims that sustainable community is achieved through patient relationship building and neighborly care.

3. Incarnation or presence in a community is an important aspect of engaging in mission. CCDA sees this principle of living in the community as essential. That is how we share all aspects of living, this is how we re-neighbor our communities. Presence in public places, sharing in what is happening is essential to relationships and community building. If the community is not good enough for us, how is it good enough for others. So, relationships or re-neighboring are pivotal building blocks. The biblical reminder of this is from John 15: 15: (TEV) "I do not call you servants any longer, because a servant does not know what his master is doing. Instead I call you friends..." That changes everything. Being a friend means presence, means knowing the other person, means reciprocity, means "hanging in there."

What do we as Christians bring to the secular vision and effort towards the City We Need?

As Christians, we have a set of values that affirms all are made in the image of God, that everyone is important. So, we bring the sense of inclusion, of working for the good of all, of balance between interests, of a commitment to the common good. In effective community organizing, we are told to identify the self-interests of all participants and move from there. But as Christians we are driven beyond that towards a vision of the common good. So often governments and social orders become unbalanced, tilted towards acting on behalf of the powerful and wealthy. We can help bring the balance.

As Christians, we also have staying power. We are in the struggle for beloved community not for our own good or greed, but because God calls us to be about the work of community, to "do justice, love mercy and walk humbly..." (Micah 6:8) And that call brings with it God's .commitment to be with us in the struggle if we make sure we are on God's side and not fall into the trap of thinking that God is on our side. So, we will work in the gap, we will work beyond our self-interest, we will stay at the table to forge solutions and sanity in the efforts.

What propels Christians to hold this vision? Where does our calling come from?

God has called us to be repairers of the breach, to rebuild the walls for the whole City. Nehemiah heard the call. He set out to repair a destroyed city. He brought together the previously marginalized, powerless people of Israel so they could analyze the issues, determine their own solutions and then implement actions to carry out the solutions. He involved the whole community. A great example of many people getting involved each having their own section of the wall to build (even the women).

We are called by God to be community builders with a vision for healthy sustainable communities and cities. Isaiah 58 shares that vision pointing out the need to combine both justice and compassion as the way to healthy, sustainable communities. Such work will give witness to God.

If you put an end to oppression, to every gesture of contempt, and to every evil word; if you give food to the hungry and satisfy those who are in need, then the darkness around you will turn to the brightness of noon. And I will always guide you and satisfy you with good things. I will keep you strong and well. You will be like a garden that has plenty of water, like a spring that never goes dry. Your people will rebuild what has long been in ruins, building again on the old foundations. You will be known as the people who rebuilt the walls, who restored the ruined houses.

Isaiah 58:9-12

References

UN Habitat (2016). *The City We Need (2.0): Towards a New Urban Paradigm.* Nairobi, Kenya: Urban World Campaign.

Lupton, R. (2011). *Toxic Charity: How Churches and Charities Hurt Those They Help*. San Francisco: Harper One.

Corbet, S. & Fikkert, B. (2014). *When Helping Hurts: How to Alleviate Poverty without Hurting the Poor.* Chicago: Moody

Von Gronnigan. *Tools-Archive*. Retrieved July 28, 2017 from https://cfapartners.org/page/Tools-Archive.

Mathie, A. & Cunningham, G. *From Clients to Citizens: Communities Changing the Course of their Own Development.* Coady Institute. Nova Scotia.

Barrett, A. *ABCD: A Theological Reflection*. Church Urban Fund. Birmingham, UK.

Websites to explore

http://abcdinaction.org/#

https://resources.depaul.edu/abcd-institute/Pages/default.aspx

www.CCDA.org.

A Biblical Theology of Land & Ownership

8

Viv Griggs

This chapter is an edited version of Ch 8 of Grigg, V. (2016). *Kiwinomics: Conversations with New Zealand's Economic Soul.* Auckland: NZ, Urban Leadership Foundation.

Land ownership is the foundation of Capitalism. It is a critical step for the urban poor to move from the lower circuit economy to the formal economy. How do we develop a Biblical theology of land ownership? The scriptures have little to say about corporate ownership or intellectual property rights per se. Which raises the hermeneutical question of the potential to realistically extend the Biblical ownership principles into these domains. The derivative theologies of property rights have a long history through the British legal system, and on into international law. These principles can be confirmed however, their application requires exploring specific business ethics and practices in each of these areas of ownership.

A house is usually our first appreciating asset. Those societies that have clear land rights and simple processes of adjudication most rapidly utilize the wealth base of society. Capital formation is not easily done unless one can buy their own home and land. We are indebted to De Soto who has demonstrated that land tenure is a singularly important element in bringing the poor into urban society and in giving them a basis for engaging in the capitalist endeavor underlying global advances into industrialization (De Soto, 2002).

Today, 1.4 billion people in global mega-cities are illegal, living on land not their own, they are known as squatters, landless people, dispossessed twice. First, they have become landless through increased exploitation by the rural rich. In the process of growing world urbanisation, an income differential has been increased between the land-owning wealthy, and the poor. Losing even the little land they have in the rural areas, many flock to the cities where they seek another foothold, a small piece of land on which to build a little shack, a little piece of security. But since the processes of gaining title can take many years. De Soto graphs the scores of steps in various cities, indicating for some 13.8 years, for some five times the income of a small business etc. For a second time, they are dispossessed of rights, and identified as illegal. In some countries, they are thus non-persons.

These are the people among whom, along with some amazing saints, I have lived for long seasons and worked for 40 years. In our struggles for land for squatters, I began to understand my Maori brothers' and my Pakeha ancestors' struggle for land in my home country of New Zealand. I will reflect on this as the framework for developing a theology which must be central to any ministry among today's urban poor.

A Crucial Pastoral Issue

Land rights is the fundamental pastoral issue for millions in these cities. Their importance has been recognized throughout the recent UNHabitat discussions by the use of the concept of "land tenure." "Land rights" are often impossible to solve, but an intermediate stage where some degree of resolution means the poor will not be evicted, enables house construction and hence asset formation. Without it people experiencing poverty in cities have little hope of ever moving out of their squalor and destitution. With it comes the possibilities of home ownership and the dignity this brings to a man and his wife; of jobs created by such housing development and of children growing up in dignity and health.

> *I see the splatter of blood on the walls of a community of squatters in which I once lived. Madame Imelda Marcos sent in the marines to move the people off her son-in-law's land. Two were murdered, seventeen wounded. This tragedy could have been prevented by reasonable talk, responsible consultation, and wise planning for development in the city.*
>
> *As a spiritual leader, had I been wiser, perhaps I could have had a role to play in laying a long-term web of relationships that would have precluded such bloodshed. Sometimes there are sins of omission that cost lives, making us as guilty as those whose sin leads them to commit murder. This issue of land is one of life and death, and it is one where a faulty theology has led to our non-involvement as Christians. That has led to the countless suffering, poverty and death of millions we could have rescued had we but studied the word of God.*

A Crucial Issue for Cultural-Spiritual Revival

Our nation of New Zealand has as one cornerstone in its formation a treaty drafted between the leaders of two peoples, freely entered into by its signatories. Central to the issues of the treaty were a mutually advantageous agreement trading overall sovereignty to the land for protection of land rights. This occurred as Pakeha (shiploads of mostly poor from Britain and Scotland), who had been dispossessed of their land by the Enclosures, arrived seeking land. They were graciously welcomed by the Maori people (the *tangata whenua*, people of the land) who in many places had a healthy economy and social structure.

The identity and *mana* of the Maori people is related to the land and hence to this treaty. To the Maori, this treaty was essentially a covenant with spiritual significance, signed in the context of encouragement from spiritual leaders. The failure of successive *Pakeha* governments to effectively uphold and honor this treaty in letter and spirit has been perhaps the most significant factor in a sense of lost dignity and caused a long turning away from the gospel by the Maori people after 90% had come Christians in two people movements (Tippett, 1971).

The battle for the soul of the Maori people is occurring today. Central to it is reconciliation and restitution of injustices over land rights. If the church is central in the process of redressing injustice, it may have the privilege of both strengthening the image of God within the soul of the Maori people and of laying the groundwork for the return of the Maori people to serving the living God.

The Theological Context

Starting with this historical context, gives us the entrance point to a theological process, which I have labelled a Transformational Conversation (Grigg, 2009). Out of the pain, we ask questions and in response create theologies. What are the issues? The right to stay! The right to own! The right to sell! The rights of landowners in mega-urban contexts.

We must oscillate from the realities and traumas of the urban conversations about terrible oppression and murder over the land of the poor, to biblical conversations on the land, the law and the rights of the poor.

Land issues are never non-emotive issues of right and wrong. Land is never just dirt but is always dirt in the context of meanings inherited from historical experience.

LAND=DIRT + HISTORY + EMOTION

Through over thirty years of teaching a theology of land rights, I have reworked Brueggeman's approach of three movements in his classic *The Land* (1977), extending them to five. In the scriptures related to the land, each has a motif of movement towards a promised land. The first is one of dispossession. The next three movements are followed by possession. The fifth is a movement yet to be fulfilled, a pilgrim people looking forward to a holy city.

Biblical Conversation about Land: Five Movements

Landlessness		Landedness
1. The cursed farm	←	The blessed garden
2. Abraham looked for a city (a sojourner)	→	Gifted the promised land
3. Slaves in Egypt, wandering in the desert, place of hard work	→	Entering the promised land, place of milk and honey, blessed, productive land
4. Exile (displaced, alienated, lost, identity)	→	Return to the promised land
5. Jesus chose to have no place to lay his head, mobile, apostolic, looking to the promised land	→	The promised city, where all have mansions, 1 cubic mile, the place of rest

We can track from the loss of a garden to the hard work of farming; to Abraham wandering in search of promised land; from slavery in Egypt to the exodus with its promise of land; to its possession and management, and mismanagement resulting in its loss. The story repeats itself finding a promise in the midst of exile, then moves to a subsequent repossession of the gifted land. Yet the promise remains unfulfilled, and a Messiah lifts our eyes yet higher to another land to possess. Meanwhile we walk as strangers and pilgrims and exiles on the earth awaiting this blessed hope.

Within these movements there is some puzzlement for pilgrim Christians as to how to identify with the Old Testament attitudes to the land. This is surprising since land is the fourth most frequent noun in the Old Testament (2,504 times) (Martens, 1981). The difficulty is because of the lack of focus on land in the New Testament. A development of these themes based on the theme of the Kingdom of God, beginning in Genesis, is helpful to clarify the unity of land themes in both testaments.

These Biblical conversations require us relating to the global and national conversations, the urban conversations, and the major literature about ecology and developmental issues, particularly agricultural land reform. The New Zealand conversations include particular concerns related to Maori – Pakeha land issues. But over the last two decades there has been a *tsumani* of complexities as New Zealand lands have been sold to foreign owners, many with no linkage to the land except for exploitation and profit. Looking globally, we need to remember conversations in each city have a particular history.

The Nature of Land

Genesis 1-3 contains the seeds for the themes of the scriptures, the philosophical perspectives around which the rest of the scriptures expand. It begins with the relationship of the kingship of God to the land. *In the beginning God created the heavens and the earth…* By virtue of God's creation of the land he owns it. Thus, in the first verse in the scriptures we have a fundamental statement as to land rights.

The land was created *good* (Gen1:4,10,12,18,21,24,31). It was also created *fruitful* (Gen1:12,22,28). It is through this fruitfulness that real wealth is created, and continues to grow. The total amount of wealth in the world is not static. Nor is it created by increasing paper money. It has a definite growth rate in proportion to the use of natural resources and their replenishment.

But this fruitfulness is directly related to the *blessing* of God. And that blessing is in some mysterious way related to humanity's obedience to God. Creation was not made independent of humanity. When Adam fell into sin the land was cursed (Gen 3:17-19).

Similarly, all except one of God's covenants with humanity are in relationship to the land. The implication is that ministry among the urban poor cannot be effected without attention to the issue of rights to their land - that their knowledge of God is intimately connected with their relationship to the land.

> *Madam Imelda Marcos arrived in a series of limousines. The people were all gathered on the basketball court. She spoke and each family was given a rolled up piece of paper representing their new title to a small plot of land. (the real paper would come later) I have seen how, almost overnight in my slum in Manila, as the community received rights to its land, the spiritual environment was transformed. Men ceased gambling and drinking and started investing money into their houses. Women and families gained security and there was a positive thankfulness to God that emerged in the midst of the sound of hammer and concrete mixing.*

The Maori relationship to land in New Zealand, as with the relationship of other tribal societies is far more closely akin to this biblical theme than the Pakeha or other Westernized cultures. To the Maori, this land was not just a commercial asset, but had a spiritual dimension. It was *turangawaewae*, a place to stand, an acknowledgment of identity and status.

The land and its produce are *good things* and part of God's command

Spirituality and the Land

While God is our final environment, we can only know him in the spatial and temporal forms of his creation.

Our spirituality is defined by our connection to the land. Our ecology is a significant factor in our spirituality.

to mankind to *manage the earth*. The management of these resources through agriculture and manufacturing also results in industry and banking. We may become rich through the wise use of these resources as God's managers, but it is God who made them *fruitful*. This relationship is not one purely of cause and effect but of a personal creator with his creation. Leviticus 26 is a beautiful chapter showing this interrelationship at a national level. We see *God's blessing* of mankind's work and the fruitfulness of the land. Elsewhere we are commanded to:

> Beware lest you say in your heart 'my power and the might of my hand have gotten me this wealth. You shall remember the Lord your God for it is he who gives you power to get wealth.
>
> Deuteronomy 8:17-18

This concept of blessing is a mystery to secular businessmen. How can prosperity be gifted? Surely, it is earned? The mystery remains. It was gifted to satisfy, as a good land, a land of bread and honey, of vineyards and trees, cities and houses, and cisterns of water (Deut 8:7-10). This was in contrast with the demanding land of Egypt, the land of effort with no reward, the land of coercion and slavery. The difference was the blessing and grace of God.

The fruitfulness of the land, and its inherent goodness is disordered as a result of the rebellion and fall but there is no evidence that its essential goodness is destroyed. Moreover, creation is not created to stand still, but to develop and grow. In fact, one could say that though creation is good, part of its goodness lies in what it can become, in the process that God has initiated (Dyrness, 1982). That fruitfulness expands wealth and is the basis of the Biblical affirmation of global urbanization.

Mankind then, is to manage this land and its fruitfulness on God's behalf for the well-being of their brothers and sisters, for from the outset the cry of "Am I my brother's keeper?" refuses to remain silent as it echoes from the hills and valleys of history. *The land is not independent from issues of social responsibility*. It is from the land that Abel's blood cries out its reply. Indeed, elsewhere the scriptures indicate that immorality and the shedding of blood bring a curse on a land.

Promised Land

When we meet Israel, it is a nation without land on the way to a promised land. A landless folk and a land of promise. The patriarchs are known as sojourners who are looking for a land.

Sojourner is a technical word usually described as a *resident alien*. It means to be in a place, perhaps for an extended time, to live there and take some roots, but always to be an outsider, never belonging, always without rights, title or voice in decisions that matter (Brueggemann, 1977). But it is not a *refugee*, fleeing, with no hope of a future. A sojourner has an acceptance and a purpose. A refugee did not want to leave, nor is there a place they left for.

Abraham, renowned because of always *looking for a city yet only seeing it from afar*, finds a land, sojourns in it, but dwells content that he has an heir to bring about the fulfilment of the promise of possession. Abraham could be called the first squatter. For the fulfilment took place by degrees. We find Jacob his son, as he is about to die, asking that his body be carried to the promised land from Egypt, recognizing a promise given yet unfulfilled (Gen 50:5-14).

So too, for the billions of migrants to the cities of the third world these last seventy years, possession has been by degrees. They too look for a city as a centre of hope, and little by little find their foothold, often content to know that though they themselves dwell in miserable poverty, their children will possess the land of promise.

In their case, the promise is not a covenant from God. Or is it? Is there inherent within the nature of the God-man-land relationship a fundamental law that all men are entitled to a plot of land for a house? Is it inherent within the nature of man's relationship to man, woman's relationship to woman, that some land be apportioned for every person and their basic needs be catered for?

Graced Economics

We are to manage on God's behalf, but that management is not sufficient for fruitfulness. There is an element of grace, an element of giftedness, an element of undeserved blessing. Similarly, we find the land gifted to Israel.

It is generally recognized by governments as a basic right for a family to own their own piece of land for a home and be able to obtain the basic necessities of life. As such, might we not say it is promised by God? Not promised with exact boundaries and area and geographical precision, nor with a *now* time frame. But then neither was Abraham's hope fixed with clear boundaries and his time frame was determined through the dark brooding of a prophetic dream about four hundred years of slavery.

The hope of Abraham was not based on any right he had to the land. Other tribes already had laid claim to it. The land would be his because it was gifted by God to him. Thirty-nine times in Deuteronomy assertions about the land as gift occur (Martens, 1981).

So too for the squatters. Due to colonial policies of land exploitation in most countries, a few families own the land in each city. Any change in this legalised oppression will only appear to the poor that the Lord has given them the land as a gift.

The initiative is with God, so we need to encourage our people to fall on their knees before God and seek his blessing. For this they can freely ask since the goodness of such a gift is inherent in his being, in his own creative relationship to mankind and creation, in his purposes for the dignity of man and woman.

Yet such prayer does not mean a passive inactivity concerning legal rights. There are many factors to be considered as a basis for land rights, and human action working along with divine grace is needed –both at he grassroots level among the poor, and among the elite urban planners and wealthy.

The land is beyond Israel's power to acquire. The defeats of Kadesh-Barnea and Ai are sufficient evidence of this. This does not mean they sit back and do nothing. Preparations are made, battles are engaged. But it is God who directs and who gives victory. So too squatters need leadership, and techniques required for success in the struggles for land rights. But it s God who is the giver of the land.

Ownership and Management of the Land

srael was not only sojourner, there were long periods where they were anded people. The sojourners become possessors.

God Owns the Land

Before their entrance into the land, Moses pauses and gives instructions about the land. Many of the principles related to the land are given in the eaching on the Jubilee in Lev 25:8-34.

n the midst of them, we find that God owns the land. Hence men are only to be God's tenants on the land, God's stewards or managers on his behalf, free to share in the fruits of his crops but answerable to him. He s the title-holder.

Private, Family, Clan and Tribal Ownership

oshua apportions to each clan and each family of Israelites a portion of and, a family inheritance (Josh Ch 13-19). This indicates God's blessing on both private and family/clan/tribal ownership of the land (where we are using ownership in the common sense of the word, recognizing that ultimately God owns the land).

Maori tribal and clan structure is anthropologically in the same category as the Israelites of this period. The land belongs to the tribe (*iwi*) and was well defined. There was no such thing as unused, ownerless land, merely different forms of land use. The *hapu* (sub-tribe, clan), the *whanau* (extended family) and the individual might have hereditary rights to its use, but ownership was ultimately vested in the iwi. This differs from the tribal and clan structure of Israel where both communal and family land rights were recognized. The difference is cultural. The Biblical principles involved are an affirmation of both communal and individual ownership patterns within a tribal or rural society.

It also differs from the Maori understanding when the Pakeha arrived. The concept of land as a commodity which could be exploited through resale, was new to the Maori. It was clear however that Maori accepted the concept of total alienation of land rights through sale only after considerable experience (Orange, 1987). Much of the land was stolen.

The scriptures are consistently strong on maintenance of legal boundaries. Deut 19:14 and other passages tell us what many government officials need to learn - never to remove the ancient boundary pegs. If we do, their Redeemer is strong; he will plead their case against us (Prov 23:11). We need to respect private and communal property rights.

Today both Pakeha and Maori in New Zealand are involved in redressing this situation and effecting restitution. If you read the Waitangi tribunal introduction to its report on Orakei *marae* you will find an excellent analysis of the injustices that occurred to this tribe concerning their land through the last century and adjudication of responsibility, analysis of what restitution is needed and what is practical.

Restitution in most situations in life cannot be exact, for acts of evil carry consequences that are irreversible. Time moves on. Restitution needs to be symbolic and real in terms of present economic realities. For the Orakei *marae* this involves the equivalent of what the land used to mean - resources for economic life for the youth of the *hapu* or sub-tribe.

Limitations to Private Ownership

God is not a capitalist, nor is he a communist. Ownership is not unlimited nor absolute. Nor is ownership to be invested in the state alone. Private ownership has validity but it is bounded by the needs of others to use the earth's resources.

In the Jubilee, which occurred every fifty years, this land was to be given freely back to the original owners so that the development of social classes through a few men gaining control of much property could not occur. God does not want society to be polarized into rich landowners and landless peasants, where "the rich get richer" and "the poor get poorer."

The Lord gave the command to let the land lie fallow every seventh year. This is an initial principle that has been interpolated into the theory of ecology. Exploitation and destruction of lands and foliage is a violation of our roles as *stewards*. This *rest* is also talked of when they were considering entering the promised land. it was to be a land of promised rest. Rest from harassment, from enemies, from sojourning, a place called home, a place of physical security. How much do the squatters need a place of such rest? The psychological stresses of living under plywood and galvanized iron, with rats nightly visiting and garbage uncollected next door cause the poor to cry out for rest! How they need the rest of freedom from harassment by landowners and politicians!

But are we correct to blithely apply these Jubilee practices to our day? What differences in the practices outlined here are demanded today as we interpret the scriptures into a mega-urban society in secular semi-capitalist states? Certainly, the fifty years of the Jubilee would not be enforceable. We have to look at the principles behind the practices - they are cross-cultural. Two principles are significant: periodic land reform in third world societies as they seek an equitable redistribution of the imbalances

Ownership Limited by Social Responsibility

Forest lands, oil lands, mining lands among others are so critical to the needs of total societies that absolute rights to these and capitalistic exploitation is not beneficial to the good of the country as a whole. They are contrary to the principle of social responsibility.

of colonial exploitation and the necessity for periods of economic reform within the capitalist system. Continuous economic growth without planned periodic redistribution is not part of God's program for society.

Related to this jubilee we may infer that cancelling of debts and liberating slaves are both insufficient acts in agrarian contexts if they are not correlated with the return of land, the means of production of wealth. Perhaps this was part of the failure of the attempt to give African-Americans land and a mule after the American civil war, it was not sufficient to produce sustainable wealth.

Urban Land

Notice Moses' clear differentiation between agricultural lands and urban land. Houses within cities were not to be subject to redistribution. After a year during which they could be redeemed, they could then be sold in perpetuity. The meaning of land in the city is clearly different to the meaning of land in the countryside. For in the country the land is seen as representative of the fruit of that land, and measured in worth according to the number of crops before the next jubilee. The land in the city had no such relationship per se to the production of wealth.

The question for our day thus becomes; What is the meaning of land in the city? and In what way can that meaning be related to just and equitable earnings and distribution of wealth?

The answer does not necessarily coincide with the legal definitions of land rights. Legality does not mean morality. We stand before a set of higher laws than the laws of nations, which are often made by rich elites with entrenched interests in maintaining control of land. The question is one of justice with equity not just of legality.

The questions are necessary questions for societies other than Israel that have many migrant populations. Migration does not lend itself to the static allocation of land as demonstrated in the early agrarian days of Israel. Increasing movement and ethnic interrelationships require different definitions and uses of land.

A further troublesome issue when we consider this issue of social equity in regard to use of urban land is the conflict between the clarity within the scriptures of God's commitment to relative equality between men and the sociological reality that cities apparently exist by exploitation and inequality.

The story of the glory of the Kingdom under Solomon is an illustration of the rapid stratification of society as a correlate of urbanisation. The commitment of God against class structure (inherent in James' teaching for example), coupled with his commitment to urbanisation per se, as the direction of history would indicate that urbanisation without stratification is a possibility and a worthy goal. But social equality is not a realistic possibility in a city unless the majority of people can freely own their own homes.

The opposite is generally the case. We can go back to the scriptures to see a case study in injustice that is echoed throughout the earth. The land of promise soon became the land of problem. Guaranteed satiation dulls the memory of the voice of God that has led them to this land and gifted it to them. The covenant that is part of the gifting is soon forgotten. Kings and the upper class soon turned it into a land of oppression and slavery as predicted by the prophet Samuel. Israel tried frantically to hold on to the land against outside enemies. As the society developed into a commercial urban society under the hands of Solomon and his sons, the jubilee was evidently not maintained. The rich became richer; the poor became poorer. It became a coercive society where:

> The ones who have made it, the ones who control the

> machinery of governance are the ones who need not so vigorously obey. They are the ones who can fix tickets or prices as needed, the ones before whom the judge blinks and the revenue officer winks (cf. Micah 3:11). It is the landless poor and disadvantaged who are subject to exacting legal claims of careful money management, precise work performance, careful devotion to all social jots and tittles, not only the last hired, and first fired but first suspected and last acquitted (Brueggemann, 1977).

The people soon forgot that fulfilled covenantal responsibility is integral to land tenure. Harlotry and shedding of blood defile the land. (Lev 19:29; Num 35:29-31). Blessing follows obedience, cursing and deportation follows disobedience (Deut 28). The gift, the tenancy agreement, had conditions. For today's poor, the conditions remain.

The Prophet's Critique of Exploitative Land Owners

Into this arena step the prophets with bold denunciation of those who trample on the poor to acquire more and more property:

Woe to those who join house to house,
who add field to field,
until there is no more room,
and you are made to dwell alone
in the midst of the land (Isa 6:8).

They covet fields, and seize them;
and houses and take them away;
they oppress a man and his house,
a man and his inheritance (Micah 2:2).

It is from these kind of prophetic statements that we find an emotive imperative for defending the squatters against the exploitation and attacks of the upper class.

The prophets both denounce such acts and cry out for men of God who would protect these poor. They denounce creditors who foreclosed mortgaged houses and fields, and high officials who confiscated more crown lands than the king had given them, exorbitant interest rates on loans which led to quick and cruel foreclosure, resulting in self-enslavement and enclosure of property (Deut 24:6; Ex 22:25).

> *Last month I visited my comrade, the mother of a family, who fed me as a young missionary learning Tagalog in a slum in Lipa city, forty years ago. They were offered the opportunity to buy a house lot. They did so, but as her husband drank, their money was insufficient to pay their monthly payments. I sent one of my team to calculate what they owed. She discovered there was interest, and fees on the interest and interest on the fees. The government were charging them around nine times what they should have been. We paid off the house, the fees, the interest. Some government officials were likely living in expensive houses!! But we rejoiced!!*
>
> *Her husband, my friend, drank away the mortgage - urban ministry is never simple.*

Extending this principle into today, we see destruction of farmlands, warfare, overpopulation, and the tentacles of urbanisation and stratification as they reach out to exploit the countryside. The result is a growing class of hundreds of millions of permanently dispossessed, landless people. Though our vision may only become fulfilled in that holy city, we must struggle for a reallocation of land for these poor.

This statement implies the right to housing. The effort to bring this to pass conflicts with the utilization of land in the city as a commodity. Thus, one role of leadership within cities is to make ways for equitable distribution of land and ownership. Yet that has to be done within the framework of the specialisations of production and distribution and their implication for land values that are endemic to the modern mega-city.

Urban economics and urban planning have fields that reflect on these ethical issues. A fertile place for Christian theologies to develop and be disseminated within those disciplines globally.

Exile: The Loss of a Land

The Sabbath and the land are quite closely intertwined in the Old Testament covenants. The prophets denounced the breaking of the Sabbath, for a Sabbath-less society reduces the nation to a smoothly functioning machine and thus its people to cogs within that machine. The machine raises a producer - consumer consciousness that denies the image of God as the core of a person's being. The Sabbath, on the other hand, sets limits to our most frantic efforts to manage life, so we remember we are the creature, not the ruler.

In judgment on these sins of Sabbath-breaking, of injustice, he takes away their land, the symbol of the covenant. The great themes of the exile relate to the loss of the land. And a question of despair echoes through their songs and laments. Does loss of the land of covenant mean loss of the God of the covenant?

Return from Exile

Jeremiah answers: even in this process, there is a renewed covenant that they will return to the land. And beyond the covenant are glimpses of a far greater covenant, and of a city to be seen only with the faith of their forefather Abraham. In the return from exile the new covenant concerning the land is made (Neh 9:36-38). This covenant is now based on a new moral management of the land.

It is this thrill of return to the promised land that we can best relate to the task of working for squatter land rights in the two thirds world, for migrant housing, for expansion of low income housing in New Zealand. Nehemiah is perhaps the best model for mobilizing a people to action.

His experience and that of Ezra and the other prophets of this period deal with the fears, the uncertainties, the group dynamics, the leadership skills needed as people dispossessed of their rural land seek to possess unused urban areas. Alinsky converted this story into the fundamental principles of community organizing.

But even in the return to the land there is no dramatic development in the Israelites' walk with God. So finally prophecy ceases from the land. The land waits. Creation awaits the coming of the Word.

Jesus and the Land

A major issue for theologians is the lack of continuity of the Old Testament with issues of land in the New Testament. With Jesus' mission, a dramatic new relationship to the land is evident. The issue of the restoration of Israel and the land disputes in Palestine is outside the mandate of this study however, others have debated this well, see McDowell, *Israel: Five Views on People, Land and State.* While the covenants remain regarding the specific people of Israel and their specific homeland, the Old Testament covenant regarding the land of Israel is now expanded with a new covenant which looks forward to a new land of promise that is not bounded by ethnic concerns, a land for every tribe and people and tongue. The themes of the exodus and exile are reiterated with renewed vigor. Again, believers find themselves as pilgrim people living by a promise, *looking forward to a heavenly city whose builder and maker is God.* In the process, many are encouraged to follow the master who chose to have *no place to lay his head* in order that he might proclaim this far-off land.

Does this mean a loss of commitment to the principles of management and social responsibility in the Old Covenant? Not in the least. The old was not abrogated. It was fulfilled and expanded to include the nations of the earth in fuller realization. Precisely because we are exiles and pilgrims with no possessions of our own we are able to help the dispossessed to gain their possession. In looking towards a future Kingdom, we are eager to pray and act towards that Kingdom being manifest within the societies of earth. And that future Kingdom comes replete with a promise of a home, something every squatter and migrant and dispossessed person understands.

We must go forward to that promise. And in the process we must bring to fulfilment the promises of God to the poor. Promises that wherever the kingdom flourishes they will possess the land that is their birth-right stolen during colonialization or political oppression by the national elites. In the process, we may frequently fail but because our eyes are fixed on a future Kingdom, we are free to bring hope, free to proclaim a more glorious home, one not built with hands, one that will not disappear or fade away. Let us go on to proclaim that hope in the midst of sharing in the struggles of our brother poor.

All of this conversation on land rights was not too complicated to imagine when New Zealand was a sovereign nation. But as $27 billion of the nation's government assets including fishing rights and forest lands have been sold off over the last decade, we face a significantly more complex set of issues. The pressures of global capitalism create market forces in most capital cities and large cities globally that rapidly escalate land prices and exclude the poor from any possibility of ownership.

Based on these principles, we can explore global evangelical practices of engagement in land rights struggles in solidarity with the urban poor and in partnership with good people of all religious backgrounds. Resources for this struggle are available at http://www.urbanleaders.org/655LandRights/.

References

Brueggemann, W. (1977). *The Land.* Philadelphia, PA: Fortress.

De Soto, H. (2002). *The Other Path: An Economic Answer to Terrorism.* New York, NY: Basic Books.

Dyrness (1982). *Christian Apologietics in a World Community.* Eugene, OR: Wipf & Stock.

Grigg, V. (2016). *Kiwinomics: Conversations with New Zealand's Economic Soul.* Auckland, New Zealand: Urban Leadership Foundation. A powerpoint presentation can be accessed at http://www.authorstream.com/Presentation/vivgrigg-2509956-theology-land-rights/.

Grigg, V. (2009). *The Spirit of Christ and the Postmodern City: Transformative Revival Among Auckland's Evangelicals and Pentecostals.* Lexongton, KY: Emeth Press & Auckland, New Zealand: Urban Leadership Foundation.

Martens, E. (1981). *God's Design: A Focus on Old Testament Theology.* Grand Rapids, MI: Baker Book House.

Orange, C. (1987). *The Treaty of Waitangi.* Wellington, New Zealand: Allen and Unwin.

Tippett, A. (1971). *People Movements in Southern Polynesia.* Chicago, Il: Moody Bible Institute.

The Gospel & the Future of Cities: A Call to Action

9

Lausanne/WEA Creation Care Network
Micah Global
The Urban Shalom Society[1]

Group statement edited by Chris Elisara

Introduction

Throughout this book, we have explored aspects of creating urban shalom from community development to land use, urban design to empowering youth and the important work of neighboring with those living in urban slums. We have attempted to demonstrate the complexity of the urban environment and yet at the same time show God's absolute love for people living in urban communities and his desire for them to flourish.

This final chapter is in a way a summary and a sending out. It's more than that though, those of us who were in Quito during October 2016 began work on the following statement, it has morphed and changed since then, yet its essence and focus on urban shalom remains the same. Our prayer is that the statement will encapsulate and make accessible a uniquely Christian response to the complex array of issues in cities. And that it will enable us to establish robust partnerships with others of good will in our neighborhoods, communities and cities so that we may work together towards God's beautiful picture of urban shalom.

The Statement

> Now the LORD God had planted a garden in the east, in Eden; and there he put the man he had formed.
>
> Genesis 2:8

> And your ancient ruins shall be rebuilt; you shall raise up the foundations of many generations; you shall be called the repairer of the breach, the restorer of streets to dwell in.
>
> Isaiah 58: 12

> Also, seek the peace and prosperity of the city to which I have carried you into exile. Pray to the LORD for it, because if it prospers, you too will prosper.
>
> Jeremiah 29:7

> And I heard a loud voice from the throne saying, "Look! God's dwelling place is now among the people, and he will dwell with them. They will be his people, and God himself will be with them and be their God... No longer will there be any curse. The throne of God and of the Lamb will be in the city, and his servants will serve him."
>
> Revelation 21:3 & 22:3

History and Intent of the Call to Action

There are times in history when it is imperative that God's people come together to pray, seek discernment and act. Such a time was the gathering of evangelical Christians convened by the *World Evangelical Alliance (WEA)* and *Micah Global* for the *Gospel and the Future of Cities Summit* October 15 – 16, 2016 in Quito, Ecuador.

The gathering was crucial for several reasons. The first was the need to build on two seminal evangelical declarations—the Lausanne Movement's 2010 *Cape Town Commitments*[2], and the 2012 Lausanne/WEA Creation Care Network's *Creation Care and the Gospel--Call to Action.*[3] We reaffirm the *Cape Town Commitments'* statement on cities that "We must love our cities as God does, with holy discernment and Christ-like compassion, and obey his command to 'seek the welfare of the city', wherever that may be."[4] The *Gospel and the Future of Cities Summit* especially wanted to take seriously the concomitant charge that "Church and mission leaders worldwide [should give] urgent strategic attention to urban mission."

We also reaffirm the *Creation Care and the Gospel--Call to Action*'s statement pertaining to cities recognizing that "rural and urban design and living" has a significant practical bearing on how to care for creation. We especially wanted to take up the statement's bold challenge to undertake more detailed work to provide in-depth guidance for Christians in this area.

Inspired by these earlier statements; as witnesses to the enormous spiritual, social, economic, and environmental challenges posed by today's rapidly urbanizing world; and in response to the prompting of the Holy Spirit; the intent of this call to action is to motivate and activate the whole church to more deeply understand, love, and care for cities and their inhabitants from God's perspective, and to become better equipped and effective for urban presence, ministry, work, and witness.The broader world is also challenged by the future of cities in these times. It was this urgency that provided the second reason for convening the *Gospel and the Future of Cities Summit* in Quito. Immediately following the summit was *Habitat III*--a global conference on urbanism organized every twenty years by the United Nations that in this instance drew together over 45,000 global leaders.[5] The document that was produced through the *Habitat III* process, and signed by all the member governments of the United Nations and is entitled *The New Urban Agenda.* Its call for more sustainable, resilient, safe, equitable, healthy, and inclusive cities, was an historic moment worthy of the church's attention and encouragement.

Indeed, *Habitat III* galvanized a moment for the global evangelical community to join the world and come together to pray for the world's cities, and to discuss and reflect on biblical truths as they apply to cities, integral urban mission, and care of creation in today's historical context. The outcomes of *The Gospel and the Future of Cities Summit* provided a platform for evangelical delegates attending *Habitat III* to engage in global dialogue about urbanism from an evangelical perspective undergirded by the consensus generated at the summit. Because the gospel applies to all aspects of life and creation, including the wellbeing individuals and communities can derive from living in cities; and because evangelical Christians faithfully following the gospel have an historic and abiding concern for cities and their inhabitants, and thus the world's urban future; Habitat III was not an event for Christians to miss.

Our Summit drew together theologians, scholars, pastors, Christian leaders, architects, urban planners, community organizers, and creation care practitioners from around the world under the auspices of the World Evangelical Alliance (WEA), the Lausanne/WEA Creation Care Network, Micah Global, and the Urban Shalom Society. ***This is a call to action for Christians to engage with urban challenges and opportunities, including UN-Habitat's New Urban Agenda.***

Our Convictions

Our discussion, study, and prayer together led us to the following two convictions.

> ***Concern for all forms of human urbanism — be they large aggregates such as cities, or smaller aggregates such as towns, villages or neighborhoods — truly is a gospel issue within the lordship of Christ.***[6]

We reaffirmed this primary biblical truth concerning cities articulated in the *Cape Town Commitment*, but also sought to explore and expand biblical understandings of urbanism with the following reflections.

God is a Placemaker

In the book of Genesis, we learn God created the earth as a good place, and thus a good home for all God's creatures. Creation, then, is a loving gift from the hand of God, and humans--who are a special and unique part of creation being made in God's image--are given the inimitable responsibility to be good and faithful stewards of God's gift of creation.

In Genesis chapter 2 we also learn God intentionally "planted a garden in the east, in Eden" for Adam to dwell. That is, God purposely made a *place* in creation for Adam and his descendants to inhabit and flourish. Some essential truths we learn from the book of Genesis include that God created people to have a relationship with Him, to live in community and right relationship with others, and to live *in-placed* lives. In other words, *people and places go together!*

This theme is reflected throughout Scripture and is particularly important for the Israelite nation as they enter in to the promised land. Later, even in exile God's command to His people is to settle in the land where they have been led, and to work for its prospering (Jer 29).

The incarnation is also an example of God's place-making desire as he seeks to make a home physically with his people. Finally, in Revelations chapter 22, we see heaven coming to earth, in the form of a garden-city. This realization points to both the importance God places on the physical environment in which we live as well as his desire to place-make with us.

God Loves People, Places, and Cities

Because God created and loves in-placed people, God is concerned about the places where people live their lives--which today are modern forms of farms, villages, towns, and cities situated within, and dependent upon, the larger gift of creation.

The character and quality of these places--which people are responsible for designing and building--have a direct impact on the wellbeing of human families, individuals, and communities. Furthermore, the design of human settlements also affects the integrity and health of the earth's ecosystems, which humans and all other creatures are dependent on for life.

Christians need to be concerned about the design of cities, towns, and villages. Indeed, it is a legitimate, abiding, and imperative concern for Christians because in God's created order people and places are inextricably tied together. Furthermore, because God is concerned that people dwell in places that are fit for human flourishing, so too should Christians be concerned with the suitability of cities for human flourishing and care of creation.

> ***The world is facing a period of rapid urbanization which is exacerbating serious social, economic, cultural, ecological, and spiritual challenges that must be addressed through integral urban mission in our generation.***

This conviction led to these additional reflections.

The Future of Cities

God's relationship with humanity starts by dwelling together in the Garden of Eden. Following the fall and restoration of all creation by the means of God's love and grace through the death and resurrection of Jesus Christ. The biblical history culminates when God and humanity once again dwell together in righteousness in a perfect place. That perfect place described in the book of Revelation is a *Garden-City* on a redeemed and renewed earth.

Cities are complex. Their designs and inner-workings can produce many positive things and bless people's lives. At the very same time city realities can grind people up and cause pain and despair. Cities can also cause excessive pollution and transgress the ecological integrity of creation, or they can function within the limits of healthy ecosystems.

Cities will never be perfect places until Christ returns, but in the meantime Christians can pray for, and work toward, designing and making cities that are just, equitable, productive, safe, diverse, healthy, ecologically sustainable, beautiful, enjoyable, etc.-- in short, places that are commensurate with God's love and goodness. In such places families, communities, and individuals can flourish.

We also recognize that while 50% of the world's population currently lives in cities, with rapid urbanization 70-75% of the world's population will live in urban areas within 20-30 years. This rapid rate of urban growth creates a fresh, insistent reality that unequivocally calls for an extraordinary response of Christian love and integral mission that is ample and sophisticated enough to respond to the challenges of rapid urbanization and the complexity of the city.

We affirm the great work of many evangelical churches all over the world as they engage with their neighborhoods, villages, towns, and cities being sources of light, life and hope. We recognize, however, that to fully participate in God's reign on earth, and the flourishing of individuals and communities in our generation, we need to go deeper into embracing, understanding and influencing the physical, social, spiritual, and other inner-workings of the city.

A Call to Action – Urban Shalom

Based on these two convictions we call the whole church, in dependence on the Holy Spirit, to respond radically and faithfully to love and care for places--cities, towns, villages, and neighborhoods worldwide, as participants in, and agents of God's shalom though the transforming love and power of Christ. We especially call on evangelical leaders, national evangelical organizations, and all local churches to urgently understand, learn, and act at personal, community, national, and international levels to "seek the peace and prosperity of the city," or what we term urban shalom.

Specifically, we call for:

- Digging deeper into scripture to learn more truths related to citie from God's perspective and to implement what we learn.
- Applying principles of biblical shalom to develop a vision and practice for urban shalom in integral urban mission. We articulate some principles of urban shalom below.
- Coming closer to God through prayer and other spiritual discipline so that along with the empowerment of the Holy Spirit we acquire Christian virtues and other spiritual resources to uphold us in ou integral urban mission work.
- Supporting, encouraging, and collaborating with our Christian colleagues who are also engaged in integral urban mission work.
- The creation of the common good through seeking to work with our non-Christian colleagues, incorporating the best thinking and practices for city-building from them and other organization devoted to improving cities. This includes, but is not limited to the work of the United Nations Human Settlements Programme otherwise known as *UN-Habitat*, and the principles of urban design outlined in the *Charter of the New Urbanism*.

Urban Shalom – Some Principles & Practices

Urban Shalom is a Vision for the City

We recognize God has a picture of the way life should be, and this pictur includes cities. Shalom—which is the picture of the way life should be best equates with flourishing and is concerned with the wellbeing of th individual in the context of their community. Flourishing includes ou basic needs being met; a sense of belonging to the land and to each other the ability to contribute to the common good; living a life full of meaning the chance to celebrate; and a growing relationship with God.

Passages such as Isa. 58:6-12, 65:17-25, Jer. 29:7, Lk4:16-20 and Rev. 22:1-5 put this concept into the context of cities, showing that they can be places where the young and old are valued, needs met, and each is engaged in meaningful work. These passages also point to the role and responsibility people of faith have in developing cities of shalom.

We affirm the concept of shalom as not only a guide for our involvement in integral urban mission, but it compels us to dialogue and work with non-Christians who are working for the common good in cities.

Urban Shalom Invites a Fresh Call to Discipleship

This vision of shalom cannot simply be another ideology to hold other leaders, government and people to. As Christians, we ourselves must become people of Shalom, more closely following, joining and participating with the Prince of Shalom. As Christians, we recognize that we have fallen short of what God requires of us in seeking cities of shalom. We have not given our whole hearts and lives to seeing all relationships flourish. We have not spent enough time sacrificially praying and standing in front of the Lord on our cities behalf. We recognize that activities that undermine God's Shalom – excessive consumerism, greed, and competitiveness, to name a few examples – are deeply ingrained in our lives and can only be transformed through Jesus Christ in the power of the Holy Spirit. We ask for God's forgiveness, and seek repentance. We ask God that the church today could become a "sign, instrument and foretaste" (Newbigin, 1989, p.233) of God's coming shalom in the places where we are responsible and have influence. ***Given the times we live in, the call to encounter, follow and join the Risen Jesus afresh as Prince of Shalom in his mission in the world could not be more urgent and important.***

Urban Shalom Embraces Economic Equity and security

God's Shalom is absent wherever people are not flourishing with God, other people and the earth. We recognize this time in history is one where cities see a growing and scandalous gap between rich and poor. Condominiums with helicopter pads and swimming pools can sit right next to overcrowded slums with open sewers. Disparity destabilizes urban relationships and our life together, dehumanizing people and destroying creation. Jesus came to "bring life and all its fullness," which is a promise for every urban resident, not just the wealthy ones. Where there are powers and evil forces at work perpetuating disparity and economic injustice we call for prayer and active opposition while working for economic equity and security for all people. This includes overcoming disparity in the spheres of business, education, media, government, art and entertainment, families and religion. Each sphere has unique challenges and opportunities to seek the shalom of the city. ***Given the growing inequalities between rich and poor, and the suffering and instability this is causing the planet, the need to confront the powers causing economic disparity while working for economic justice, equity, and security for all people is vital and urgent.***

Urban Shalom Embraces Diversity

Cities are by their very nature diverse places. Indeed, a city could not function if every person had exactly the same talent, or was the same age and gender. We therefore, welcome diversity in all its complexities, recognizing that Christians can be people of welcome and hospitality, helping neighbors belong together despite differences. We recognize that no individual church or Christian group will be able to respond to all the diverse challenges and opportunities of their city. Strategic alliances, therefore, need to be developed that can: share people, resources, and expertise; identify emerging trends and find responses in pro-active ways; help to advocate for specialist, yet connected responses. ***Given the expanding cultural and religious diversity of our cities, and the needs for***

human dignity and respect for diversity, the role of shalom-makers and community builders is vital and urgent.

Urban Shalom Cares for Creation

Creation is a gift from God that has an ecological integrity which supports life. God calls us to be good stewards and caretakers of His creation, thereby enabling us to enjoy the fruits of creation to meet our needs, but not overstepping the ecological limits of creation and destroying the fruitfulness of creation.[7]

The everyday intersection of most people's lives and God's creation is not a pristine forest, a wild river, a tropical reef, or some other unspoiled part of creation, but their home and the city or town it is a part of. Thus, how cities and towns are designed and built; how they function internally (e.g. their transportation systems; their drinking water, waste water, and storm water systems; their energy systems; their solid waste systems; etc.); how they relate to their neighboring rural/agricultural communities; and how they relate to wild places--land, rivers, lakes, oceans, etc.—has a big impact on the health and integrity of creation. For this reason urban shalom requires that urban development uses models and practices of urban land use, city planning, architecture and design, and building that comports with preserving the ecological integrity of God's creation.[8]

Urban Shalom Involves Urban Design

One of the defining characteristics of the urban context is high densities of people sharing a common place. How this sharing of place is negotiated is a crucial challenge for faith and mission. Given the speed of urbanization the burgeoning of quickly established slums and informal settlements, suburban sprawl, and tower block sprawl is understandable, but can undermine human flourishing. The role of imagination, designing, planning, and building places amenable to humans living together in harmony with God and place is therefore a critical one. The Judeo-

Christian tradition recognizes that seeing urban shalom happen in cities requires deep prayer, imagination, will, and political engagement coupled with commensurate urban design and development. ***Given the growing density of populations and the various types of stresses this is causing, the need to design, develop, and where necessary retro-fit places so they comport with shalom so communities can flourish, is vital and urgent.***[9]

Urban Shalom Engages the Public Square

Christians are explicitly called to be "salt and light" in the world, thus we have a responsibility to contribute to the common good of the city, which requires proactively and constructively engaging in the public square.

We lament that as evangelicals our engagement in the public square has not always come from a place of love, and has not always born witness to God's Kingdom or his shalom. It is with regret that we acknowledge the times we have stood in the way of God's purposes in the world, through ignorance, institutional self-interest, individual divergent priorities, or other motivations.

Because of this recognition we seek to enter the conversation around the future and development of cities with a humility and an openness to truly hear the perspectives and needs of others living in, and served by the city, and where possible to partner on initiatives. We recognize that we don't have to control initiatives but simply serve, bringing what we have to offer to the table.

We also acknowledge that many people of faith are already in positions of influence within cities, and as leaders we pledge to encourage and strengthen those leaders to be bearers and influencers towards shalom.

Urban Shalom Develops Relationships and Collaborations for the Common Good

Jesus encourages us to seek out people of peace and to work with them for he benefit of the Kingdom. In a rapidly changing world we acknowledge he need to do this like never before. We seek to develop relationships and collaborations with others who may not share the faith but who are open o its values and the possibility of working together toward the common good. This will allow us to connect with their expertise currently outside of our reach and influence its use towards shalom.

We also recognize the value of organizational partnership, and will seek o build connections between churches and local authorities, educational nstitutions, international organizations and so forth for the positive levelopment of the city. These include, but are not limited to the work of *JN-Habitat*, and the principles of urbanism outlined in the *Charter of the New Urbanism* and accompanying *Cannons for Sustainable Architecture and Urban Design.*[10]

Associations for the Common Good of People, Places, and Cities

As people of faith we are not starting from scratch in this endeavor. We have a long history of relevant cultural engagement that reflects Gospel nd Kingdom priorities in cities. From starting hospitals to running chools, to service agencies and NGO's that work all over the world oving, strengthening, and building up the resilience of marginalized people living in cities. We also recognize that people of faith are not the only ones concerned about cities and the experience of people living in hem. In October 2016, fifty thousand people gathered in Quito, Ecuador or UN-Habitat III. They were city planners, architects, leaders of NGO's, politicians, support agencies, academics, activists, advocates, UN officials, ngineers, climate specialists, all with the aim of creating sustainable and vable cities.

Drawing on the Biblical narrative, including the concept of shalom, as well s our own history and learning, we recognize there are three important xtra-biblical international documents that Christians should be aware of nd analyze for the data and information they contain, the practical tools

and insights they offer, and the strategic goals they describe regardin
cities and their development over the next 20-30 years.

The City We Need 2.0: Towards a New Urban Paradigm[11] was put togethe
through a civil society consultation process involving 26 Urban Thinker
Campuses held in various places around the world. The outcome of thes
conferences and other meetings identified 10 key principles for cit
development.

Cities need to:

1. Be socially inclusive and engaging
2. Be affordable, accessible and equitable
3. Be economically vibrant and inclusive
4. Be collectively managed and democratically governed
5. Foster cohesive territorial development
6. Be regenerative and resilient
7. Have shared identities and sense of place
8. Be well planned, walkable and transit-friendly
9. Be safe, healthy and promote well-being
10. Be places of learning and innovation

The second document is *Habitat III's New Urban Agenda.*[12] This documen
was unanimously ratified in Quito by all member nations of the Unite
Nations at the culmination of the conference. It drew heavily on th
recommendations of the *City We Need*, as well as expertise from othe
key stakeholders. We affirm its core vision;

> We share a vision of cities for all, referring to the equal use and enjoyment of cities and human settlements, seeking to promote inclusivity and ensure that all inhabitants, of present and future generations, without discrimination of any kind, are able to inhabit and produce just, safe, healthy, accessible, affordable, resilient, and sustainable cities and human settlements, to foster prosperity and quality of life for all. We note the efforts of some national and local governments to enshrine this vision, referred to as right

to the city, in their legislations, political declarations and charters.

The third, and very practical document, is the Congress for the New Urbanism's *Charter For The New Urbanism* that opens with the following statements that then lead into specific urban design principles. We affirm the Charter's core understanding about cities and principles for urban design.[13]

> *We view* disinvestment in central cities, the spread of placeless sprawl, increasing separation by race and income, environmental deterioration, loss of agricultural lands and wilderness, and the erosion of society's built heritage as one interrelated community-building challenge.
>
> *We stand* for the restoration of existing urban centers and towns within coherent metropolitan regions, the reconfiguration of sprawling suburbs into communities of real neighborhoods and diverse districts, the conservation of natural environments, and the preservation of our built legacy.
>
> *We recognize* that physical solutions by themselves will not solve social and economic problems, but neither can economic vitality, community stability, and environmental health be sustained without a coherent and supportive physical framework.
>
> *We advocate* the restructuring of public policy and development practices to support the following principles: Neighborhoods should be diverse in use and population, communities should be designed for the pedestrian and transit as well as the car, cities and towns should be shaped by physically defined and universally accessible public spaces and community institutions, and urban places should be framed by architecture and landscape design

> that celebrate local history, climate, ecology, and building practice.
>
> *We represent* a broad-based citizenry, composed of public and private sector leaders, community activists, and multidisciplinary professionals. We are commit- ted to reestablishing the relationship between the art of building and the making of community, through citizen-based participatory planning and design.
>
> *We dedicate ourselves* to reclaiming our homes, blocks, streets, parks, neighborhoods, districts, towns, cities, regions, and environment.

Whilst these documents are holistic in nature, as people of faith we must ask the question; *do they go far enough towards manifesting a Kingdom of God (shalom) agenda in the world?* We proffer this question not out of contentiousness, but sincerely from our commitment to Christian faith as we engage with these globally influential events and documents related to the world's urban future. Where compatibility and common good can be found we will undertake supportive actions implementing the *New Urban Agenda.* And where from a Christian perspective we see deficit in the *New Urban Agenda* we are willing to take divergent actions tha we believe are in line with advancing God's vision for urban shalom. We apply the same to the *Charter for the New Urbanism* and the Congress for the New Urbanism that works to advance the design principles of the charter.

A Call to Action is a Call to Prayer

A call to action requires more than words and activities. There is a spiritual struggle over the future of the city that we must not shy away from. We especially encourage prayers for:

- **Engaging Reality**: Lord, open our eyes, ears and other senses to perceive what is happening in our cities, towns, and villages. Help us to find ways to appropriately respond to the realities we perceive and understand.
- **Lamenting Grief**: Lord, help us feel deeply what you feel about the happenings in our cities, towns, and villages. We especially pray for forgiveness where we have been responsible for, or benefited from, holding others back from flourishing in our cities, towns, and villages.
- **Finding Hope**: Lord, our hope is in you and the redemption of all things in Christ (Col. 1:15-19). Help us to be your agents of shalom in cities, and for cities. May we be fully empowered for this work by your Holy Spirit, the truth of your Word, the vision of your Kingdom on earth, and the assurance of Jesus' return that will consummate the reconciliation and redemption of all creation, including cities, that was initiated with Jesus' resurrection victory over sin and death.
- **Celebrating Victories**: Lord, help us to rejoice and celebrate the breakthroughs and victories—big and small, that will be won along the way as we take up this call to action for urban shalom.

Agreed together by the participants of the Gospel and Future of Cities Summit, Quito, Ecuador, October 16, 2016.

Notes

1. Formally the Urban Shalom Project

2. To review the *Cape Town Commitments* go to: https://www.lausanne.org/content/ctc/ctcommitment

3. To review the *Creation Care and the Gospel-Call to Action* statement go to: http://www.weacreationcare.org/wp-content/uploads/2015/04/Call-To-Action-Word-Doc.pdf

4. Cape Town Commitment II.D.4.

5. The objectives of *Habitat III* were to "secure renewed political commitment for sustainable urban development, assess accomplishments to date, address poverty, and identify and address new and emerging challenges" and to produce a "concise, focused, forward-looking, and action-oriented outcome document." The document that was produced through the *Habitat III* process, and signed by all the member governments of the United Nations, is entitled *The New Urban Agenda.*

6. For convenience sake, we will refer to the range of human settlements - cities, towns, villages, etc., simply as "the city." For example, when we affirm that "God loves the city," what we really mean is God loves not just cities but all variety of places - cities, towns, villages, etc., that people design and build for human settlements.

7. For more in-depth information about the principles of creation care this call to action upholds and supports go to: http://www.weacreationcare.org/milestone-wea-statements-on-creation-care/

8. The *Charter for the New Urbanism* and accompanying *Cannons of Sustainable Architecture and Urbanism* articulate principles and practices that can be used to design and build places that care for creation. To read these documents go to: https://www.cnu.org/who-we-are/charter-new-urbanism

9. The critical relationship between urban shalom and urban design applies not only to care of creation, but many other aspects of shalom in the city. Thus, the *Charter for the New Urbanism* and accompanying *Cannons of*

Sustainable Architecture and Urbanism apply practically to this point too. To read these documents go to this link: https://www.cnu.org/who-we-are/charter-new-urbanism

10. To read *The Charter for the New Urbanism* and the accompanying *Cannons of Sustainable Architecture and Urbanism* go to: https://www.cnu.org/who-we-are/charter-new-urbanism

11. To review *The City We Need 2.0* go to: http://www.worldurbancampaign.org/sites/default/files/documents/tcwn2en.pdf

12. To review *The New Urban Agenda* go to: http://habitat3.org/wp-content/uploads/New-Urban-Agenda-GA-Adopted-68th-Plenary-N1646655-E.pdf

13. To read *The Charter for the New Urbanism* and the accompanying *Cannons of Sustainable Architecture and Urbanism* go to: https://www.cnu.org/who-we-are/charter-new-urbanism.

Contributors:

Dr. Ash Barker

Immersed Jesus activist, trainer, writer, speaker. After 25 years of urban mission in Melbourne and Bangkok, Ash with his wife Anji and son Aiden moved to Winson Green, Birmingham, UK, to live in residential community. He founded Newbigin House, Newbigin Community Trust and Newbigin School for Urban Leadership. Ash is from Melbourne where he helped start and led *Urban Neighbours of Hope* and the *Surrender Conference*. For 12 years he and his family lived and served in Bangkok's largest slum. Ash speaks widely, is the author of eight books and has a passion for raising up more resilient, urban Christian leaders.

Dr. Chris Elisara

Chris is an educational pioneer in Christian higher education, an entrepreneur, award-winning filmmaker, and an urbanist. After growing up in New Zealand Chris moved to the United States where in 1996 he founded a Christian undergraduate environmental study abroad program with campuses in Belize and New Zealand. In 2010 he founded the Center for Environmental Leadership before being invited in 2012 to found the World Evangelical Alliance's Creation Care Task Force. In his WEA role Chris works with UN-Habitat, the World Economic Forum, and other international agencies. Chris served on the board of the Congress for the New Urbanism (CNU) from 2013-2016 and has produced several award-winning films on urban topics.

Prof. Bryan McCabe

Bryan is Pastor of Transformational Urban Leadership at North Way Christian Community in Pittsburgh, Pennsylvania. Through this role, he provides leadership with the LAMP mentoring initiative, the House of Manna faith community, and the Transformational Urban Leadership Institute. Bryan also serves as a professor of urban missiology at Bakke Graduate University.

Evelyn Miranda-Feliciano (Deceased)

Evelyn was a resident writer and former Executive Director of the Institute for Studies in Asian Church and Culture. She was a best-selling author who had been recipient of various awards and citations, one of them the Catholic Mass Media Award. Previous to her work in ISACC, she and her husband David, a theologian, were full-time faculty of the Philippine Missionary Institute, which trains pastors and church workers in grassroots communities. A gifted teacher, she has trained writers and spoken in various forums not only in the Philippines but in countries across the Asia region. She is survived by her husband and two sons.

Dr. Viv Grigg

Viv has been a prophetic voice, living among the poor, church planting in Manila, Calcutta, Sao Paulo, Los Angeles and Auckland. He has catalyzed several new apostolic orders (networks of communities) who live incarnationally in the slums of over 40 emerging mega-cities. He currently coordinates he Encarnação Alliance of Urban Poor Movement Leaders, that networks over 45 slum movements. He is also a speaker, rainer and Urban Missiologist, gaining qualifications in missiology and theology from Fuller Theological Seminary. He teaches on Citywide Leadership, Transformation and Revival Movements, Church planting, Ministry Among the Urban Poor and Postmodern Urban Transformation. He has also authored numerous books and currently serves as Director of the Urban Leadership Foundation.

Michael A. Mata

Michael has led and equipped others in community and church-based urban transformation for more than 30 years. He is director of the Transformational Urban Leadership Graduate Program at Azusa Pacific Seminary. Michael also serves as Community Transformation Specialist for Compassion Creates Change, Inc., and was the director of Tools for Transformation for World Vision's U.S. programs. Prior to his time with World Vision, he held the Mildred M. Hutchinson Chair in Urban Ministries at Claremont School of Theology. He has nearly 20 years of experience in urban pastoral leadership, and holds degrees in biblical literature, religion, and urban planning.

Dr. Christopher Miller

Christopher is professor at Judson University near Chicago and lectures, consults, and facilitates student research in sustainable buildings, places, and communities. He also leads students in field studies of exemplary walkable cities.

Dr. Mary Nelson

Mary has spent over 50 years in faith-centered community development in a low income, African American community on Chicago's west side (where she also lived and worshipped). She has pioneered creative efforts around affordable housing, economic development, and community building. The faith focus and empowering approach built on the strengths of people enabled significant results. She later became President of the Parliament of the World's Religions, and helped lead them towards a successful international Parliament event of over 10,000 people in 2015. She teaches at the Asset Based Community Development Institute at DePaul University, is a conference speaker and active in justice and environmental issues.

Andre Van Eymeren (PhD Cand.)

For the past two decades Andre has been involved in grassroots community development. Engaged in everything from caring for at risk young people, to running community wide celebrations. Most recently merging church and community development, in the outer South East of Melbourne. Post this experiment he formed an organization that aimed at training and equipping the Church to better engage the world around it. Resigning at the end of 2014, he is now reflecting and building upon that practical experience in his writing, teaching and facilitating. Andre is also a researcher at Swinburne University focusing on the biblical concept of Shalom as a model for building social infrastructure in cities, where people can thrive and flourish.

CPSIA information can be obtained
at www.ICGtesting.com
Printed in the USA
BVOW06s0813290917
496291BV00011B/70/P

9 781999 779894